Interesting Women of Jefferson City

Michelle Brooks

With Carrie Mackey Hammond

[signature]

11/8/2022

DEDICATION

This book is dedicated to resilient women who make the best of whatever circumstances and opportunities befall them.

CONTENTS

ACKNOWLEDGMENTS

The Zonta International is a leading global organization of professionals empowering women worldwide through service and advocacy. One of the major projects of the Zonta Club of Jefferson City is to provide a second-chance scholarship program benefitting women who desire to begin or the intent of acquiring an education and skills necessary to enter or advance their status in the workplace.

Since 2001, the local club has helped hundreds women with its Second Chance Scholarships.

This program is supported solely through gifts and the annual Yellow Rose Luncheon, which was postponed due to COVID-19 in 2020 and 2021. A portion of proceeds from this book will directly benefit the scholarship fund.

1 RUTH RUST

Once the Only Female Photographer of State Officials in the Nation

- ❖ Born: June 23, 1887, Holden, Missouri
- ❖ Died: March 26, 1957, Jefferson City, Missouri
- ❖ Notable: Official photographer for legislature, state officials

An adventurous woman and an innovative entrepreneur, Ruth Rust operated her own photography studio for decades in downtown Jefferson City. At one time, she was the only woman in the nation to be a state's official photographer.

Although she provided a feminine touch inside her studio and was particularly skilled in working with children's portraits, Rust also served the Missouri legislature and state officials from 1925 to 1944.

She provided space at her studio, upstairs at 210 E. High St., in the Dallmeyer building, for women's groups to meet and hold exhibits. And, she wasn't afraid to stand up to the system and challenge city laws.

Rust arrived in Jefferson City in 1921, when she bought the studio operated by Ed Ford and Thomas Jack Simcoe. [i] It is likely, Simcoe contacted Rust after she ran an ad in Abel's Photographic Weekly: "All-round photographer would like position in studio which could be bought later; or to rent studio which would later be for sale. Town of 5,000 or more. Central states preferred." [ii]

Simcoe, a Fulton native, had been a student at Westminster College in the 1880s, before operating photo studios in Chillicothe and Jonesboro, Arkansas. After 1910, he came to Jefferson City to take over the studio, which had been recognized as the "official studio of state officers and legislators" for the majority of the years between 1885 and 1935. [iii]

Like Simcoe, Rust operated photo studios in several cities.

She was introduced to photography by her older sister, Jennie, who left the family home in Buffalo to study photography in Holden, where the children had been born, and later with a Mrs. Tackett in Coffeyville, Kansas. Jennie Rust then moved to San Antonio, Texas, where their older brother, Byron, helped to get her a job with the A.A. Brack Studio. In 1901, Jennie Rust bought the Powell Studio in Beeville, Texas, becoming the first woman photographer in South Texas. [iv]

Ruth Rust experienced failing health while in high school in 1904. So, her parents sent her from Buffalo to live with her sister, Jennie, in Texas. [v] There, she took up photography. By 1910, she had returned as a photographer in Buffalo. She moved to Montezuma, Iowa, in 1918, where she quickly bought the photo studio of Z. Swearingen. [vi]

A few years later, the 34-year-old arrived in Jefferson City. One of her first ads in September 1921, said: "Miss Ruth Rust, the photographer, has made a special study of photographing the little folks and has the necessary patience for this work."[vii] Within a few months, she also added a Kodak photo finisher, allowing next-day pick up for customers at 132a E. High St., which she shared with Miss Ruby M. Weeks. [viii]

When she arrived in 1921, other photographers included Weeks, Carl F. Deeg, 225 ½ E High St.; Racker's Studio, 304 ½ E. High St.; and Thomas G. Cooper, 2 Merchants Bank building.

She was "ever alert to the new possibilities in her chosen vocation" the newspaper said.[ix]

In 1923, the local newspapers had not yet added photography to their regular design. Many of her portraits were featured on the society pages of local ladies announcing weddings, anniversaries and positions within organizations. She also took photos of dance troupes and organizations. The Kansas City Star, even, picked up some of her work.

When the Jefferson City Post Tribune added a new engraving plant in June 1935, its Pictorial Progress edition featured many of Rust's photos, along with those of Deeg and other local photographers of the time.[x]

Her studio already had seen more than 50 years of prestige in the Capital City when she walked into 210 ½ E. High St., or the second floor of the Dallmeyer Building. [xi]

The location first was the studio of F. Gustave Suden, remembered for his 1890 Souvenir Sketchbook. Immigrating from Holstein, Germany, in 1871, Suden opened a gallery in St. Louis and then was an itinerant artist before opening his studio in 1878 in Jefferson City.[xii] He became the photographer of the General Assembly in 1885 and continued until he moved to Texas about 1902.

The Dallmeyer Building studio passed to L.F. Miller by 1904, then to Edwin P. Ford by 1908 and finally, after 1910, to Simcoe. So, Rust adopted a legacy for quality photography and a standard high enough for state officials.

Among her competition, was the Rackers studio was opened by P.H. Rackers by 1908 at 203 ½ E. High St. and moved to 304 ½ E. High St. by 1921, when Mrs. Clara Rackers was in charge. And Thomas Cooper began operating out of the Merchants Bank building before 1921.

Jefferson City-born Carl Deeg studied with Suden at 125 E High St., before establishing his own studio in 1888 at 225 E. High St. and continuing operations for 50 years. The son of German immigrants, he was popular with the Commercial Club, Merchant's League, Elks, Eagles and the Modern Woodmen.[xiii] He and his wife, Elizabeth Sommerer of Honey Creek, lived and hosted boarders at their 1908-built home, 210 W. Dunklin St.[xiv]

After three years in business in the Capital City, Rust was featured in the Kansas City Star's Women in Business column. The headline called photography an "ideal business for women." [xv]

Although her business was booming with state officials, candidates and notables visiting the Capitol, Rust "takes the most pride in handling the business of women and children," the article said. "Miss Rust's studio is distinctly a man-less affair. Her employees are women; and the decorations of the studio and furnishings are suggestive of the feminine." [xvi]

Her work with children began with youngster photos, extended to Girl Scout Camp lessons in outdoor photography and included the Jefferson City High School yearbook, the Marcullus. [xvii]

"The quality of photographic work produced by Miss Rust and her capable assistant, Miss Anne

Ruth Rust. Photo generously provided by Sidney S. and Martha Dugat of Beeville, Texas.

Milliken, won recognition throughout Central Missouri and has also played an important part in winning laurels for the local school publication in contests conducted throughout the state and nation," the Daily Capital News said in 1928. [xviii]

She also worked for the Simonsenian staff to help provide a souvenir edition of the junior high school newspaper. And, Rust would provide to the public photo plates from special events, like ones of individual floats participating in the annual May Day and Health Day parade. [xix]

Milliken worked for Rust for several years before being named the county welfare agent.[xx]

Among the Capital City's women, Rust hosted at her studio the AAUW Book Hour, the Business and Professional Women's Club art exhibits, PEO meetings, and the Jefferson City Art Club shows. One of the more popular of these was an annual child photography exhibit.

Beyond membership and meeting space, Rust also took an active role in club leadership and projects important to her, like investigating the noon-day lunches provided at the city's schools.

A civic-minded entrepreneur, Rust provided weekly book reviews to the local newspaper to promote a circulating library she set up in the front of her studio in August 1936. She started with more than 50 of the latest books, available to guests with no membership fees.

"The library in the fore part of the studio includes many new books and makes a pleasant and convenient browsing spot," the News Tribune said Aug. 30, 1936. [xxi]

Rust also didn't hesitate to speak out in the male-dominated business and city government worlds. For example, W.A. Slocum did not file for a business license when he was taking baby pictures at the Millsap Store on High Street. As the trend of stores bringing in such photographers was growing, Rust challenged the city business license ordinance. [xxii]

Millsap's argued that since Slocum worked for them, it was under their business license, suggesting that otherwise, every drug store, which sold more than drugs, would need multiple licenses. However, City Attorney June Rose agreed with Rust that Slocum was operating a separate business, requiring a separate license. [xxiii]

What may be most notable about Rust's professional career is her work for the State of Missouri. She was the only woman serving as a state's photographer in 1935, and likely many other early years. [xxiv] Although she benefited from buying the established Suden-Ford-Simcoe studio, it was her own character and skill that perpetuated those contracts for future years.

She had the privilege to take the first contemporary senate photo, which was hung in the new Capitol upon moving in and it ran in the Secretary of State's Blue Book. [xxv]

Curiously, Rep. Edward M. Brady from St. Louis in 1935 declined to sit with Rust for the 58th General Assembly group picture. But, he assigned no specific reason for his refusal. "This is the first legislator in her experience to refuse to have his photograph taken," she said.[xxvi]

Today, along the limestone hallways of the Capitol, Rust's name and work remain on several house and senate composite frames.

Rust was born in 1887, the fourth of six children to Alice and Dennis Rust in Holden. Her father had served with the 9th Indiana Infantry for about 6 months during the Civil War, before being discharged due to disability. He arrived in Johnson County before 1870. And, her mother's family had moved there from Woodford, Kentucky, before 1860. [xxvii]

The Rust family of 8 moved to Buffalo in 1892, when Ruth was 5. Her father had been a drayman in Johnson County and was a grocer/truck farmer in Dallas County. After her father died in 1915, Ruth's mother moved to Texas to live with Jennie, who had married Beeville ranchman Sidney Dugat. [xxviii]

Ruth Rust lived at her studio on High Street early on with roommate and studio assistant Ann Milliken. [xxix] About 1930, she remodeled her studio in the Dallmeyer Building and moved into the newly-expanded C.L. Petit Apartments, at the corner of Madison and McCarty streets. [xxx] In addition to sleeping rooms, the home had seating for 150 guests in its dining room, serving

Photo courtesy Tim Bommel

regular meals, and the living room was the site of many community parties. [xxxi]

By 1940, Rust had moved in as one of three lodgers living with Anna Trippensee, her son and his wife, and her three other children. [xxxii] She was diagnosed with muscular dystrophy in 1948, dying nine years later, at her home at 705 Ewing Dr., of bronchopneumonia, a complication which developed while she was battling breast cancer. [xxxiii]

2 MATHILDE KATHERINE "DOLLY" DALLMEYER SHELDEN
A Woman of Society, Feminine and a Force

- ❖ Born: Dec. 6, 1885, Jefferson City
- ❖ Died: Jan. 1980, Kansas City
- ❖ Notable: Women's suffragist, influential speaker, Republican party leader

The turn of the 20ᵗʰ Century was a fortuitous time for Mathilde Katherine "Dolly" Dallmeyer Shelden to be born in the Capital City to a prominent family. She grew up in luxury, but was also encouraged to use her mind, even if her political views differed from her father's.

A woman of society, Dolly was poised and feminine. She attended the right clubs and hosted the right parties. But she also was outspoken on women's suffrage. Dallmeyer took advantage of her location to get involved with the statewide movement and she helped organize the Jefferson City Equal Suffrage League. xxxiv

She was born in 1885 to Rudolph and Louisa (Schmidt) Dallmeyer, the third of five children. Frank and Paulina welcomed their new sibling. Her younger brother by five years, Charles died as an infant. And then the youngest, Alvin, was born in 1892. xxxv

Her mother's family, the Schmidts, settled in Cole County in 1828. Dolly's maternal grandfather had been city mayor in 1871 and county treasurer. He also was a well-respected builder, with architecture including the Dallmeyer building at 206-208-210 E. High St., the Madison Hotel and 526 E. Capitol Ave. xxxvi

Dolly's father was the youngest of 9 children born in Dissen, Hanover, in 1857. Several of his older brothers had immigrated to the U.S. and had returned to Hanover for a visit after the end of the Franco-Prussian War. William Quintillian, an older brother, encouraged a 14-year-old Rudolph to join them in America. [xxxvii]

Rudolph arrived in New York in August 1871 aboard the ship Weser. His father had been a dry goods merchant in Dissen and older brother, Hermann, had established a successful dry goods business in St. Louis. There Rudolph worked five years as a clerk. [xxxviii]

In 1874, Rudolph moved to Jefferson City to become manager of the J.T. Craven & Co. Dry Goods Store at 210 High St., of which his brother William was a partner. Soon after, the Dallmeyer brothers took over the business as Dallmeyer & Co. At age 24, Rudolph opened his own company and store on Madison Street in a building erected for him by Joseph Stampfli. He moved to larger quarters in 1886, two doors down on Madison Street, in a building owned by Hugo Monnig. He incorporated his business in 1896 as the R. Dallmeyer Dry Goods Company. [xxxix]

In 1898, he enlarged his store on East High Street. He operated the "largest and most complete dry goods house in Central Missouri," the 1906 Book of Missourians said. The 12,000 feet of floor space on the main floor stretched across two addresses. Another addition was built in 1922, creating a ladies garment shop and occupying 206-208-210 E. High St. [xl]

He served three terms as president of the Commercial Club – 1901, 1902 and 1909 -- and was an original board member on the proposition to build the Missouri River Bridge. He also was a member of the Country Club and the Elks.

Rudolph met his wife, Louisa, while she worked for him at the store. The couple married in 1878 on Valentine's Day, because that was "the dull time at the store," Dolly's brother wrote in a letter to the editor in 1957 to the Sunday News and Tribune. [xli]

When Rudolph opened his own business in 1881, the couple lived above it. Later, they moved into the historic, 14-room Maple Terrace, the steamboat-inspired home built by Judge Robert Wells, who designed the Missouri State Seal. The lost home once sat on the corner of Adams and East High streets, where the Missouri River Regional Library is today. At that time, 325 E. High St., looked similar to the Governor's Mansion with a stone retaining wall and wrought iron fence at the sidewalk.

The pre-Civil War home had been at the center of social activity while owned by Judge Robert Wells, who served 10 years as Missouri Attorney General and 30 as a federal judge. Wells bought the lot in 1825 from Major Alfred Basye. The home was built in the architectural style of a river packet, with double-decked porches and spiral stairway on the front veranda. Its walls were made of weather board-covered logs, three-feet thick in some places. During the war, it quartered several officers, Wells being pro-Union. Judge Wells died in 1865, but his widow, Eliza, continued to live there.

In the 1870s, it was used as a private school then it passed through a few owners. When she was an infant, Dolly's father bought Maple Terrace in

1886 for $4,000, according to a 1935 Sunday News and Tribune.

In 1905, the Dallmeyer family moved around the corner, into a home which Rudolph had built at 214 Adams St. But the family kept possession of Maple Terrace, modernizing it into a multi-family residence. It was razed in the late 1930s and replaced with a filling station. Today, the Missouri River Regional Library sits on that corner.

Photo courtesy Missouri State Archives Summers Collection

A conservative progressive during the most crucial era of Jefferson City's history, Dolly's father was a prime mover in several civic initiatives, including the Commercial Club, the J.R. Spencer Ferry Company and, then, the Jefferson City Bridge and Transit Company, a founder of the Rotary Club, the Thomas viaduct across Weir's Creek, and the Bagnell Branch railroad. He aided in the organization of Capital City Building and Loan Association and was made the honorary president. He also served as Director of Jefferson Home Land Company and served as a second ward councilman.

The Book of Missourians said his success was "not as a result of accident, but by thorough training of his well-balanced mind, coupled with unceasing industry, impelled by an ambitious spirit, supported by an almost perfect physical manhood." [xlii]

Dolly's father was a strong influence on her; she patterned many of her steps after him. She was not single-minded in her endorsements, but lent her voice to a variety of issues and organizations over time.

Her activism started early. By age 10, Dolly was asking why she couldn't vote. And, her father nurtured her opinionated nature, even when she chose the Republican party over his Democrat party.

As a high school student, Dolly won the 1900 Illustrated Sketch Book Prize Essay for "Reasons Why Jefferson City Should Provide for Maintenance of the Library With Which Mr. Carnegie Proposes to Endow the City." The sketchbook called her "a young lady of a good mind and a charming person, who has every promise of a bright future."[xliii]

During her studies at National Park Seminary in Washington D.C., after graduating from Jefferson city High School in 1903, Dolly was introduced to the opportunities of political involvement. [xliv]

She "early displayed a leadership in civic, club and political affairs and always has been noted for her interest in people," Ford said in his History of Jefferson City. [xlv]

She was a charter member of the Art Club of Jefferson City and president 1906-1915. The art club organized in the fall of 1903 and was comprised mostly of young women of college age. Dolly founded the club with her sister, Pauline, but Alta Elsner was its first president. The organization met weekly at the public library in its early years and often hosted exhibits and lectures open to the public. [xlvi]

Dolly was also a long-time member of the Music Club, of which her mother was president for a number of years. The group met in the Executive Mansion music room with several first ladies serving as hostesses. [xlvii]

Several times throughout her life, Dolly enjoyed traveling abroad with family. When she was 19, she and older sister Pauline visited the United Kingdom. After marrying, she shared her love of travel with her step-children, Russell and Jane, taking them in 1931 to England.

None of her travels compared, though, with the 1914 trip to Amsterdam with her parents and brother Edwin. Rudolph had taken his family to visit his homeland, traveling in Europe by Pullman for safety and service. The Dallmeyers, like several other Jefferson Citians, found themselves trapped in Europe in August 1914 at the beginning of World War I. Others included Mayor Cecil W. Thomas and wife, Mrs. Fredericka DeWyl Simonsen, Jacob Moerschel and his son, Ernest.

While visiting Dissen, Hanover, Dolly and her family were in Berlin when they saw the mobilization of the German army and the celebrations of the German people at the fall of Belgian and French strongholds, the St. Louis Globe Democrat said in 1918. In total, the Dallmeyers were delayed an extra two months from returning home from Europe, which they did in early October 1914 aboard an overcrowded boat out of Holland. [xlviii]

"They did not scurry for home as most Americans did; they remained long enough to become familiar with war's fearful conditions, which (Dolly) considers one of the most educational experiences of her career," The

Kansas City Star said in August 1929. Eventually they returned to the U.S. on. [xlix]

After Dolly's mother died of ovarian cancer in 1916, her activism increased.

When the U.S. entered World War I the following year, Dolly served as the vice chairman of the Cole County Liberty Loan Committee, alongside her father who was the chairman, helping to sell $10,000 worth of war savings certificates in Hermann alone. She also helped collect $5,000 worth from employees at the International Shoe Company's 220 employees. [l]

With her father, she toured the county with an orchestra and meals prepared by farm wives. Many of the German-ancestry residents were "aghast at the large amounts of bonds to which they were expected to subscribe," brother Alvin wrote in 1957. Nevertheless, Cole County was the first of 110 counties to exceed its goal. [li]

Dallmeyer was a skilled and prolific speaker. Her war savings stamp speeches were helped by her first-hand experiences in Germany.

"Few if any, public speakers ever drew as large an audience as did Miss Mathilde Dallmeyer of Jefferson City, who spoke at the Cole County Courthouse Thursday evening. Miss Dallmeyer had been announced as the Joan of Arc of Missouri and she well deserved the honor, for, whether inspired or not, she at least completely captivated her hearers and led the biggest crowd that had ever gathered at the courthouse into an overwhelming charge on war saving stamps and brought Hermann a victorious over-subscription," the April 12, 1918, Daily Capital News said. [lii]

She applied her speaking skills to the state's suffrage movement. After arriving home from her first-hand observations of the conflict in Europe, Dolly took off on a 21-county speech tour. [liii] That meant 4-5 speeches each day and relying on whatever transportation she and her chaperone could find. "So controversial was the prospect of women voting that several times she and her chaperone were refused accommodations," Jane Flynn said in her 1992 "Kansas City Women of Independent Minds." [liv]

"A versatile, witty and magnetic speaker, she held audiences spellbound," Flynn said of Dolly. [lv]

Dallmeyer had been elected recording secretary for the Missouri Equal Suffrage Association in April 1913. Their goal was to prepare an initiative petition for the 1914 statewide ballot. At that time, 22 leagues existed across the state, including Jefferson City with 50 members. In contrast, Warrensburg had 100, Sedalia 150 and St. Joseph 60. [lvi]

The Jefferson City Equal Suffrage League invited the wife of Secretary of State, Cornelius Roach, to be the club's president in February 1913, but she declined citing the care of her 12 children and "home duties are too numerous and enacting to leave me any time to look after league affairs."

Beginning about 1870, women had been visiting the General Assembly in Jefferson City to appeal for voting rights. It is likely in the 1910-20 era, Dolly was hostess to some of these ladies before or after their presentations.

More than just speeches and petition drives, Dolly put her views into action. In May 1915, she set out to answer the question "Can a girl get along as well and be as well received socially, when she takes a job, as when she is merely a social creature?" [lvii]

To find the answer as a delegate to the Missouri Federation of Women's Clubs, she "had to get a job and the job she picked out is that of representing Lindenwood College of St Charles in a canvass of the 38 states from which that institution draws students," the St. Joseph Gazette said in May 1915. "If she isn't snubbed when she presents her letter of introduction in her own charming way and if her friends whom she last saw in Paris or London or some of the other European capitals, don't glance glassily at her when they find out that she is actually engaged in toil, then she'll know that all this talk about the working girl's position being inferior is all bosh." [lviii]

During the 1918 General Assembly, Missouri suffragists kept an open house in Jefferson City, Alice Stone Blackwell said in "The Woman Citizen." The article said Mrs. Walter McNab Miller was assisted by local women, and, no doubt, Dolly was one of them. [lix] The state's proponents benefited from the support of Gov. Frederick Gardner and his wife, another enthusiastic suffragist.

Once suffrage was passed, the work of women in politics began. Dolly was an officer in the 8th District Republican party 1919-20, chairman of the Women's County Committee, and vice president of the reorganized Missouri State Republican Club, "marking her as the first woman to hold political office in Missouri," the 1929 Kansas City Star said. [lx]

She was "one of the first women ever elected to high party place in the country," the Kansas City Times said. [lxi]

In 1919, women were invited for the first time to the Republican national conference and Dolly was a delegate in Washington, D.C. She also was part of the first Republican committees to include women at both the county and state levels. [lxii]

She was among the Republican Women of Missouri who "took their first step in politics" in July 1919, when the Women's Executive committee met with the Republican State Committee to organize and elect officers, where Dolly was passed over for the position of Women's National Executive Committee member. [lxiii]

"Republican Steam roller: Flattens all opposition – Miss Dallmeyer is punished for lead on machine method" was the May 7, 1920, Daily Capital News headline. The story's lead said "Republican stand patters never functioned so well" during the state convention. [lxiv]

Apparently, those who were used to being in charge of how the state convention works, were interrupted by Dolly's efforts. The men tried to rush through their slate of eight men for the Chicago convention with seven white and one black man. But, then, Dolly was "given credit with having smashed the plans of the bosses to ignore women." [lxv]

For her efforts, Dolly was shunned in the final nomination, although the final delegation included two women. "Many here expressed the opinion this election was a direct slap at Miss Dallmeyer because of her activity against the original plans of Babler-Cole-Kiel-Schmoll-Dickey-McJimsey-Markes combined," the news said. [lxvi]

Dolly's voice was clear and present against the "boss and machine rule," the St. Louis Post Dispatch said. "She is a young woman of most forceful personality, large of stature, with a voice of good carrying quality, a fearlessness and a wholesome frankness which inspire confidence where others must depend upon diplomacy," the Post-Dispatch reported May 9, 1920. [lxvii]

When she married Kansas City dentist Frank Elwin Shelden in July 1920, she was vice president of the Republican Club of

Photo courtesy Missouri Valley Special Collections, Kansas City Public Library, Kansas City, Missouri

Missouri and chairman of the Woman's Republican State Committee. Although she moved to Kansas City, her activities in civic work and politics continued. Like her father, her husband encouraged her activism and political work. [lxviii]

In 1924, she was appointed to fill a vacancy on the Kansas City Council upper house. [lxix] Sadly, her father was killed in a car accident while traveling to Kansas City with Dolly to see her at a council meeting. Dolly and her two step-children, a niece and the chauffeur, also were injured in the July 4,

1924, accident near Lone Jack. [lxx]

Dolly and the children had spent two weeks in Jefferson City and were returning home. Their driver attempted to pass another car, skidded on some loose gravel and overturned. Her father was seated in the front and had been thrown through the windshield. In the back seat, Dolly with Jane, 9, and Russell, 3, as well as Louise Dallmeyer, all fell against the luggage protecting them from serious injury. Russell had left his grandfather's lap for the backseat just minutes before the accident. [lxxi]

Her father had spent 43 years as a merchant in Jefferson City. "He was known for his kindness and generosity," the Kansas City Times said. [lxxii] At the time, he was president of the Central Evangelical Church board, which passed a resolution of sympathy. "In his passing we have lost an able and efficient counselor, a true and loyal member and friend," the Daily Capital News reported. He also was in the midst of his term as president of the Commercial Club. [lxxiii]

Dr. Shelden, and his brother, Homer, were both dentists. Frank was a well-known tennis player, who "held various state and Mississippi Valley championships," according to the Kansas City Star. [lxxiv] He graduated from the University of Pennsylvania School of Dentistry in 1899 and was "one of the early men to specialize in corrective dental work in this area," his obituary said. [lxxv]

He also was active in the Republican party and civic affairs, serving on the staff of Children's Mercy Hospital 25 years. He was born in Rockford, Illinois, but graduated from Topeka High School. He was a charter member of the Mission Hills Country Club, where the couple's 1.5 acre estate was located. [lxxvi]

Dolly said in a 1929 interview with the Kansas City Star, "marrying a widower with two children and adding one of my own was the biggest job I've ever undertaken." [lxxvii] Shelden's first wife, Jeanette May Smith died in December 1918 of broncho-pneumonia, leaving children Frank Copeland and Jane Kelley. [lxxviii] The Sheldens added their son Russell Dallmeyer to the family. At their home, the children enjoyed an outdoor gymnasium, a basketball goal, miniature baseball field and the nearby swimming pool.

Their son, Russell, attended the University of Missouri-Columbia, graduating in 1942 with a Bachelor of Arts and a commission as a second lieutenant through the U.S. Army ROTC field artillery. He served two years in the European Theater of Operations as a medical laboratory technician, including care for wounded from the Battle of the Bulge at the 1,000-bed general hospital in Liege, Belgium.

In 1947, Russell earned a with a Bachelor of Science degree, followed by his M.D. in 1949, from the St. Louis University School of Medicine to become an anesthesiologist. He continued in the U.S. Army active reserve with the 325th General Hospital as Chief of Anesthesiology and Operating

Room Service until 1965. Then, he returned to active duty in 1978, retiring as a Colonel in 1983.

Dolly remained active in social, club, church and political affairs in Kansas City. An inaugural member, she served as president in 1929 of the 20th Century Republican Club, with a membership of more than 1,000. The organization, which met at the Hotel Baltimore, was designed for ongoing education and fellowship. "Politics is not a thing to rest on the shelf from election to election. The science of government is a never-ending theme of interest and stimulation," Dolly told the Kansas City Star. [lxxix]

Dolly "will be remembered and appreciated for her role in serving as an advocate for women's rights," author Jane Flynn wrote. [lxxx]

She was president of the Kansas City Rose Society in 1947, a musette of the Kansas City Museum, a member of 2nd Presbyterian Church and a long-time city Republican committeeman. She served on the Council of Churches executive committee and was president of both the Browning Society and the Kansas City Dental Society Auxiliary. [lxxxi]

Other interests included the Harris Home Association. Women's Executive Committee of the Kansas City Philharmonic Orchestra, and the Women's Commission of Kansas City Art Institute. [lxxxii]

"Without a doubt, of all of our women friends who have been active in civic affairs, Mrs. Dolly Shelden has been the most prominent," George Fuller Green said in his 1968 "A Condensed History of the Kansas City Area." [lxxxiii]

3 HAZEL MCDANIEL TEABEAU
Trail-Blazing Student, Civil Rights Advocate, Exacting Professor

"She was an enigma to me. She was a brilliant woman, always self-disciplined and socially conscious."

— Dr. Thomas Pawley

- ❖ Born: Dec. 4, 1892, Fort Smith, Arkansas
- ❖ Died: May 12, 1969, Cook County, Illinois
- ❖ Notable: First African-American to earn a doctoral degree at University of Missouri-Columbia

Hazel McDaniel Teabeau challenged segregation in academics as both a student and a professor. When Lincoln University took a stand against a community parade decision forcing them to rear, she led the reactionary event. And when the University of Missouri-Columbia first admitted African-Americans to its graduate programs, she was among the first seven students, eventually being the first to earn a doctoral degree there.

"Never content to be where she was; (Teabeau) possessed an inner strength that drove her to know more, to do more, to be more. She was a liberal and politically minded individual whose interest in social causes and concern for civil rights was evidenced by her active memberships in the NAACP and the Missouri Association for Social Welfare," a magazine article said. [lxxxiv]

Teabeau joined the faculty at the Lincoln University English department in 1937, after teaching English one year at Wilberforce University, Ohio. With a love of theater, she worked with Prof. Thomas Pawley, helping act in and direct numerous plays until his retirement in 1988.

"She was an enigma to me. She was a brilliant woman, always self-disciplined and socially conscious," Pawley said. [lxxxv]

A perfect example followed an October 1942 War Bonds and Stamps event, hosted by the Roscoe Enloe Post #5 American Legion and Auxiliary and featuring Sen. Harry Truman and Cardinals baseball players Mort and Walt Cooper. More than 1,500 people participated in a parade from the library on Adams Street, west on High Street to the Capitol building. [lxxxvi]

Each community in the county was asked to send a contingent. Bands from St. Peter Catholic School and Jefferson City High School played and other entries included members of the armed forces, Civilian Defense units and school children who had participated in the salvage drives. Nearly 6,000 people attended the 7 p.m. event in near-freezing temperatures and more than $100,000 in bonds was raised. [lxxxvii]

When the 40-piece marching band and another 200 students from various organizations from Lincoln arrived to participate, however, they were told they would be at the end of the parade, with other black organizations from the community. Lincoln President Sherman Scruggs attempted to discuss a change with the parade official, a local businessman, but was met with "discourteous treatment," according to the Kansas City Times. [lxxxviii]

Parade officials later defended that the parade line up as being based on the order in which reports for participation came in from the various groups, including each town in the county, with Lincoln being the last to submit its plans. [lxxxix]

Scruggs chose to boycott the parade altogether and the other black community members followed. He later released a statement, saying: "The ready and willing enlistment of our young men into the armed forces of the nation, the serious study by our young women to prepare themselves for many areas of service in the home front and the willing sacrifice that is often made to purchase bonds and stamps by older adults and children are greater manifestations of our loyal ties and patriotism as really true Americans and good citizens of JC than marching as unwanted participants in a parade." [xc]

Instead, "Dr. Scruggs asked Hazel to organize Lincoln's own Four Freedoms March. It was our contribution to the war effort and it was quite a success," Pawley recalled. [xci] The Four Freedoms of speech, religion, from want and from fear were drawn from a recent speech made by President Franklin Roosevelt. [xcii]

The Nov. 7, 1942, Lincoln Army Day began with Lincolnites walking five-abreast in lock-step from the campus, down High Street to the Capitol. The procession was led by Army Day Queen Eunice Merriweather and her attendants, the university's marching band, a small corps of U.S. Army soldiers and Pres. Scruggs. After that were banners announcing "Education. First Line of Defense." Other banners and organizations followed, including the Red Cross, safety education, air raid wardens, home management, public health, defense classes, auxiliary policemen and firemen. [xciii]

Sigma Gamm Rho sorority organized pledge classes from all Greek organizations for the Double V project, pulling a large letter "V" on a float and members marching in the form of the letter behind. Across the nation, Double V was the term racial justice supporters used to support victory in Europe but also a victory over racism at home. [xciv]

When the procession reached the Capitol, they sang the "Star-spangled Banner" and "Lincoln, O Lincoln." Then, they marched back down Lafayette Street to the campus. [xcv]

A football game against soldiers from Fort Sill, Oklahoma, followed. At half time, acting Physical Education Director Raymond Kemp read the names of all Lincolnites in the armed services. Then, "Taps" was played for Richard Parker, the first student to "give his life in the global struggle for democracy," the Clarion reported. [xcvi]

Just six months before this local incident, Parker, a 1940 graduate who volunteered for the U.S. Navy, was killed in the bombing of the SS Lexington aircraft carrier in the Battle of the Coral Sea.[xcvii] He was a math and sociology major, who had moved to southern California to pursue a movie career.

"From that moment, the war at LU could no longer be discussed academically. Richard Parker's death 'in the line of duty' had brought the war's whole tragic import home to us," Lincoln Clarion reporter T. Thomas Fletcher wrote in 1943.

HAZEL McDANIEL TEABEAU
Instructor in English

Photo courtesy Lincoln University Archives

The next school year, Teabeau received a sabbatical to earn her Master of Arts degree from the University of Chicago. She had spent several summers advancing her education, including 1938 at the State University of Iowa and 1939 at the Chicago Repertory Theatre and Ann Rudolph School of Dramatics. [xcviii]

Teabeau resumed leadership in civic pride when she returned for the 1944-45 school year. Locally, her efforts went beyond the campus, such as a book review of Richard Wright's "Black Boy" for the Civic Pride Charity Club and being the principal speaker at Quinn Chapel A.M.E.'s Women's

Day. [xcix] [c]

At the state level, she became the first African-American to be editor of the Missouri Association of Social Welfare's monthly "Building a Better State," which had expanded its policies to include threats to civil liberties.

The next year, in February 1948, Teabeau was the first African-American speaker at a University of Missouri-Columbia campus auditorium. [ci] Authorities gave permission only after agreement that no African Americans would be in the audience. [cii]

Five years earlier, a similar request had been denied. And even one year earlier, the Unitarian Liberal Club could not gain approval for another Lincoln professor, Cecil Blue, to talk on "The New Negro." So, that program was held at Calvary Episcopal Church. [ciii]

Teabeau's barrier-breaking talk was a critique of Willar Motley's novel, "Knock on Any Door" delivered to the Unitarian Liberal Club at the Bible Institute building on the main campus. "Repeated efforts and denials had preceded the University's approval of a Negro speaker on the campus," the Clarion reported. [civ]

"If I had been invited to make a talk at the University by university officials and such conditions of audience exclusion had been set up, I would have declined. But, here I was joining a progressive student group in the interest of progress in human relations," Teabeau told the Clarion. [cv]

She agreed it was an "important first step in the direction for social and interracial progress." Hazel added: "… the break in what seemed to be unbreakable precedent … goes to the students who have for years pursued an ideal of breaking down in democratic institutions the walls of racial exclusion." [cvi]

A few months later, in May 1948, Teabeau again faced prejudice in Columbia. As vice-chairman of the Progressive Party's state central committee, she was invited to speak in advance of the arrival of third-party presidential candidate Henry Wallace at the Boone County Courthouse. [cvii]

During her speech, the crowd sang "Dixie" and she experienced "unexplained microphone trouble." [cviii] To a crowd of more than 5,000, she "lashed out at the bi-partisan government for its do-nothing policy on civil rights," the Clarion said. She warned against the domination of government by big business and militarists. [cix]

The microphone trouble extended to Wallace, whose speech was interrupted by shouts and booing. His words included: ""If we do not practice democracy here regardless of race, we cannot have any influence in the rest of the world," according to the Moberly Monitor Index. [cx]

Two years later, Teabeau was among the first 10 African Americans admitted to MU in the fall of 1950, two years after Pres. Harry Truman initiated the desegregation of the U.S. Military and four years before the U.S. Supreme Court's ruling on Brown vs. the Board of Education. The

U.S. Supreme Court in 1950 had ruled in several cases enforcing the 14th Amendment in matters of segregation. [cxi]

Teabeau had been a Lincoln faculty member 12 years, when she attended MU and also lived on its campus.

"The university has not flung wide its doors but has opened them only to the extent the law specifies. The court decision now provides that Negro students, who are residents of Missouri, must be admitted to the University of Missouri when equally good courses are not obtainable at Lincoln, the State's all-Negro university. Responsibility for deciding whether courses are equal lies with the University of Missouri," The Post Dispatch reported. [cxii]

The opportunity for Hazel and the others to attend MU followed a ruling by Cole County Circuit Judge Sam Blair, based on similar cases recently before the U.S. Supreme Court. Elmer Bell Jr. and George Everett Horne had applied as freshmen engineering students and Gus Tolver Ridgel to the economics graduate program. When they were denied, "they charged that refusal to admit them was a violation of their rights of equal protection under the 14th amendment," the Post Dispatch said. [cxiii]

Ridgel was the first African American to earn a graduate degree, graduating in 1951. During his year on campus, he said he visited with Teabeau often. "It was always relaxing and refreshing to sit and talk to Hazel Teabeau. She was a likeable person who offered me a great deal of encouragement during that period of my life," he said. [cxiv]

In the spring of 1951, 13 of the 7,400 MU students were African-American – eight men and five women, three undergraduates, five graduate students, two nursing and three part-time, according to the St. Louis Post Dispatch. [cxv] Among them was Melbourne Langford, also from Jefferson City, who was in the educational guidance program.

Teabeau's experience was different from most of these first-time African-American students on the MU campus, as she also lived in a dormitory on campus. Addressed as "Mrs. Teabeau," she was well-liked and respected by the other women in the dormitory, called the "chicken coup," said Dr. Frances Fairchild, who lived in the same dorm. [cxvi]

Discrimination could have come Teabeau's way in a second way – her age. However, the doctoral program's age prohibition was rescinded because of her brilliant classwork. [cxvii]

Her second year in the MU doctoral program, Teabeau was awarded the McAnally medal, the oldest literary prize at MU, for her essay "From the Cycle of the West." [cxviii] She had an extensive knowledge of the English language – "how to read to understand, how to write to communicate and how to speak to influence," the magazine said. [cxix] She easily could have earned her doctorate in English. But, "because of her infatuation with the spoken word, she opted to pursue a PhD in speech," the article said. [cxx]

She had "an exceptional academic record" in speech and drama, Arnold

Parks said in his "History of Lincoln." [cxxi]

Her dissertation topic on the slave trade was at the suggestion of her adviser, Dr. Loren Reid. "I wasn't sure what her reaction would be. I guess even then people had an interest in their roots because she said yes to my idea," Reid said. [cxxii]

When the time came for Teabeau to defend her 708-page "Wilberforce's speeches on the Abolition of the slave trade" dissertation, even the graduate school dean sat in on the historic moment. [cxxiii] In 1959, at age 66, Hazel was the first African American to earn a PhD from MU.

"Hazel Teabeau was a bright, motivated woman who had an interest in all subjects," Reid said. [cxxiv]

She was a "kind and caring person who deserves enormous respect for being able to hold her own and as she competed in a world dominated by men," said Carl Smith, a fellow student in the 1950s. She "was a woman ahead of her time, especially in her attitude toward the news and how it was reported. She was critical of journalists and she insisted that when reading the newspaper, you must read between the lines. Never take the newspaper literally, she'd say." [cxxv]

Teabeau "was never intimidated by a challenge. People who knew her speak of her courage, her intelligence and her unyielding drive," the magazine said. [cxxvi]

She believed one must have the desire to get along with others and speech could be used for social control. "One should take an inventory of himself to objectively evaluate others," she said at a 1953 Lounge and Learn hour at Tull Hall. [cxxvii]

Teabeau joined Lincoln librarian Freddye Thompson and sociology professor Loftus Carson to discuss the "importance of getting along." [cxxviii]

"'We must study others in terms of ourselves. Know how to say the proper thing at the proper time, when there is dissitory attitude," Teabeau concluded. [cxxix]

In addition to persuasive speech, Teabeau held a high standard for precision.

"Improper pronunciation was one of her pet peeves. If you didn't enunciate your words properly, Mrs. Teabeau was quick to correct you. She placed tremendous value on the English language and the right way to use it," Carl Smith said. [cxxx]

And Dr. Ann Smith, a student of Teabeau's at Lincoln in the late 1950s, said Hazel was "a very demanding person. If you didn't do your absolute best, it didn't count. ... Because of my experiences with her, I am constantly pushing myself to produce high performance in everything I do." [cxxxi]

Teabeau was born in 1892 in Fort Smith, Arkansas, the second of three children of a letter-carrier, Edgar McDaniel, and his wife, Emma, and by

1910, the family moved to McAlester, Oklahoma.

She had earned a bachelor's degree in English from the University of Kansas in 1915 and taught two years of high school in Oklahoma before moving to St. Louis to teach. There, she married Ralph Teabeau, a U.S. Army medical officer, in 1929.

While in St. Louis, she worked as editor of the Interracial Review, an employment agency interviewer and as a welfare caseworker. Teabeau was assistant editor of the Federated Colored Catholics in the United States Chronicle and a member of the St. Louis committee of the North American Committee to Aid Spanish Democracy.

In 1962, she moved to Ohio, teaching English and speech at Central State College two years, before returning to Jefferson City and her home at 430 E. McCarty St. She died May 12, 1969, in Cook County, Illinois.

The magazine summed up her success as that she "lived life to the fullest, driven by her own confidence, courage and convictions."

4 BELLE SIDDONS

Missouri Gal Turned Gambling Queen

By Carrie Mackey Hammond

- ❖ Birth: about 1842 near St. Louis
- ❖ Death: unknown
- ❖ Significance: Jefferson City socialite, Confederate spy, Queen of the Black Hills

It was uncommon to have a debutant lobbyist in 1866, especially one such as Belle Siddons. Known for her charm and beauty, she claimed to be the catalyst with members of government for the passing of mysterious bills, scandalous all night parties, and secretive trips to St. Louis. However, Belle's mastery of Jefferson City's elite society was neither the beginning nor the end of her story.

In a small room in Deadwood South Dakota in 1881, a woman who had just ingested a large amount of morphine, convinced a local reporter to visit her. She told him she was going to give the details of her life story, in what she believed was a deathbed confession and a wish to have her obituary properly written. This reporter was about to hear a fabulous and tumultuous tale.

Belle Siddons was born in Missouri around 1842, to a wealthy political family and raised on a plantation near St. Louis. Her family, including relative Robert Stewart, who was Missouri's governor until shortly before the Civil War broke out, were very active in the political scene. Her good looks, wit, and family associations cemented Belle as being a well-connected young woman with a bright future.

Belle's father sent her to the female Seminary School in Lexington and after graduation, she made her societal debut in Jefferson City around the start of the war. Being beautiful and distinguished, she was the object of desire for the young men who crossed her path. Especially drawn to the vivacious southern belle were the soldiers preparing to leave and join the war. The first real love for Belle was a fellow named Captain Parrish. When Belle and Captain Parrish first met, he was betrothed to a young woman from Louisiana Missouri. However, with Belle's efficient and determined manipulation skills, he eventually gave in to her charms. Captain Parrish broke off his relationship with the woman from Louisiana in order to pursue Belle. With the other woman being heartbroken, her brother challenged Captain Parrish to a duel in order to restore their family's pride. The duel resulted in a draw. Both men were satisfied with the result and agreed to go their separate ways.

Not long after this mostly nominal duel, Captain Parrish left for a military campaign. Belle had made the promise to marry him upon his return. Unfortunately, Captain Parrish did not survive his first battle engagement. This seems to be where life's tide shifts for Belle. Outwardly, she seemed cheerful and animated, with not even a hint of mourning. However, with Belle's sudden and drastic change in focus, her good nature could be perceived as a cloak for abyssal pain…with a desire to deliver justice to the North, on behalf of her beloved Captain Parrish.

Belle quickly learned that she could use her wiles to benefit the rebel cause and essentially, she became a confederate spy. She infiltrated military headquarters, spending time with love struck Union soldiers. Dancing, charming, and plying them with drinks, she spent her days and nights gathering information. She learned a great deal from General Halleck and General Curtis's ranks and discovered every major movement their soldiers were making. She passed her new knowledge on to General Forrest and the rebels.

As crafty as Belle was, she surprisingly made no secret of her duplicitous behavior. In 1862, General Curtis became aware of her shady activity and issued a warrant. Warned of her impending arrest by one of her soldier admirers, Belle wasted no time in fleeing. Unfortunately for Belle, it was not long before the authorities caught up with her near Ste. Genevieve. The authorities found incriminating maps in her possession and Belle proudly admitted to being a spy when questioned. She claimed her assistance and knowledge helped bring victory for General Forrest in some of his most notable raids.

Belle received a sentence of one year in the Gratiot Street Prison in St. Louis. After only four months, they released her, under the condition that she would serve as a nurse for the remainder of the war.

When the war ended, Belle spent her time lobbying in the Capitol City during the time of Governors Thomas C. Fletcher and Joseph W. McClurg. It was at this time she gained the reputation of using her beauty to influence legislation and encouraging members to flex their power in specific ways. This is around the same time she met handsome Kansas City surgeon,

Newt Hallet. After a short courtship, they married and moved to Texas. Belle's new husband was quite fond of gambling and taught her to play cards. He spent his days patching up patients with Belle as his nurse. Sadly, the seemingly happy marriage was short lived, as Newt died from yellow fever within two years.

Distraught from the loss of her husband and the need to support herself, Belle left Texas and made her way toward the gambling halls of the upper West. This was also when she began dabbling in drugs and alcohol.

Belle takes this time to reinvent herself again. Now known as "Madame Vestal," she

Photo courtesy Missouri State Museum

held jobs in various gambling halls while making her way north. Becoming a specialist in dealing cards, she rarely lost. For those that crossed her path, losing to the beautiful Madam Vestal became a badge of honor. She would sit silently shuffling cards at the roulette table, long dark hair cascading down her shoulders, in full costume of velvet and lace gowns, adorned with diamond and ruby jewelry, with a pistol on one side and stacks of money on the other. She ruled the gambling hall and gamblers came from every corner to pit their luck against her faro table or roulette wheel. If any disputes arose in her gambling hall, she handled them with a flash of her pistol. In telling her story to the reporter, Belle claimed that during her time in the gambling halls of Cheyenne, Wyoming her luck was invariable. She said she had a superstition that if she allowed the thought of kindness toward gamblers to enter her soul, it would break her spell of fortune and ruin her artifice for "drawing in the suckers".

By 1876, The Black Hills gold rush was in full swing. Madame Vestal decided to take a wagon loaded with gambling furniture north to South Dakota in order to open a new gambling hall. Soon after arriving in the Deadwood area, Madam Vestal's reputation gained the name "Queen of the Black Hills" and she once again set up her gambling empire.

It was not long before another man entered Belle's life, one with whom she fell deeply in love. His name was Archie Cummings, and he was a former guerilla raider. Together, they forged a plan and she once again became a spy. Archie was involved with a gang of road agents who frequently robbed stage coaches as they traveled between The Black Hills, Deadwood and Rapid City. Belle would sweet talk information out of stagecoach drivers, and Archie and his gang would lie in wait to rob the stagecoach of its valuables. Her silent and observant nature allowed for her to overhear all sorts of conversations while dealing cards. This included talk regarding road agents, from the lawmen who aimed to stop them. It was not uncommon for Madam Vestal to allow such men to win a little money at her table, in order to keep them happily talking. She was able to find out when valuable cargo was to be traveling through and when the heat was turning up on the gang. It wasn't long before Belle was not only involved with the road agent gang – but was running it. She claims she decided which coaches they were to plunder, gave advice on how to carry out each crime, and organized each robbery down to the last detail.

The road agents were increasing in boldness with the stagecoach heists, and eventually their luck began to run out. While lying in wait for an oncoming coach, the gang was surprised by a group of lawmen. Archie and another gang member were seriously wounded, but managed to escape into the woods. Belle found them and since she couldn't risk bringing a surgeon to their hiding place, she tended their wounds as best she could using her nursing skills. Before long she was able to utilize her connections to smuggle Archie and his friend into Deadwood, where they received more extensive medical care. Within a few days they had returned to their criminal habits and the lawmen were none the wiser.

Most men saw Madame Vestal as an intimidating presence, but she met her match with a bounty hunter known as Boone May. While posing as a reckless and courageous stage driver, May showed up in the area and set out to win her trust. It didn't take long for his outgoing personality and style to catch her favor. She gave up enough information to him that he was able to dispatch a group of lawmen to round up Archie and two of his fellow gang members while they were boarding a train out of town. The original plan for the gang was that Archie and his friends would leave town, with Belle joining them a short time later with the accumulated loot. Their plan was now foiled and the gang in custody. Stopping outside of Fort Laramie near Cottonwood Creek, the lawmen removed the three road agents from the coach and hung them. They used the same rope for each gang member, which required the next one in line watching the one before them strangle to death. Archie's turn was last, and he begged to be able to write his mother a goodbye letter. The lawmen agreed, with the condition that Archie would disclose the location of the gangs loot. Archie refused the offer, so the lawmen then told him that if he gave them the details of the stolen goods they would spare his life. Archie readily agreed, and moments after bestowing the information, the lawmen strung him up. After he was dead, they hung a sign on his body warning for it to not be removed.

Guilt over the death of Archie engulfed Belle. She vowed to kill May and everyone involved with Archie's death, but this never came to pass. She spent the next few years wandering the West, drinking heavily and visiting opium dens. This was the point where she ingested a large amount of morphine in order to commit suicide and contacted the reporter for what she believed to be her final chance to give her narrative. However, due to a high tolerance for drugs after years of opium use and drinking, she made a full recovery. Normally Belle was someone who loved attention, however the deathbed confession to the reporter embarrassed her. Knowing the interview would cast her in a negative light, Belle contacted the newspaper reporter and threatened to have her men "put his light out" if he published her story.

Eventually her wandering stopped in Nevada, where according to census records, she married Eugene Holman who had a young daughter. The new Mrs. Holman decided to settle down, quit drinking and focus on family life. With the help of her new husband, Belle opened a musical theatre and took on the stage name "Lurline Monteverde." She seemed to finally have her life together and things were looking up for her. Unfortunately, the good times did not last. Her theatre burned to the ground and she lost everything. The devastation caused by the fire and the loss of her dream theatre, caused her to begin drinking again.

Eugene tried desperately to pull her out of depression. Tragically, when in a drunken state, Belle hit his daughter across the face with a liquor bottle. Eugene had enough and Belle was on her own again.

Newspaper accounts of her story and census records of the last few years of her life readily exist. However, this is where truth meets legend in the life of Belle Siddons. The majority of her story comes only from her own claims and Deadwood tales. Set up for success in ways that most young women of the time could only dream of, Belle's path twisted and turned in arduous ways none of her juvenescent admirers in Missouri could foresee.

Today, if you search the internet you will find an author's interpretive sketch and a couple of black and white photographs under Belles name. These photographs feature a lovely actress who played Belle in a 1950's Wild West show. No known pictures of the real Belle Siddons actually exist nor do we have confirmation of exactly when and how she died. There have been two separate claims regarding Belle's death. One, she died from a drug overdose and another that she died in jail. We may never know how much of her colorful life story were true or the details of her death. She continues to live on through her legend, which over the last century and a half, has been the subject of many spirited Wild West stories.

5 **GRACE WOOD HERSHEY**

Skilled Stenographer made Ultimate Sacrifice to Serve her Country

- ❖ Born: 1887, Abilene, Kansas
- ❖ Died: October 1918, at sea bound for France
- ❖ Notable: Stenographer, only woman named on the Cole County World War I memorial

Grace Hershey was an outstanding stenographer. She was praised in both contests and courtrooms for her record-keeping. At age 31 in 1918, she had worked her way from retail and law offices in three states to the Missouri State Department of Insurance.

Hershey was born in 1887 in Abilene, Kansas, to Pennsylvanians William and Jennie Hershey.

At age 18, she worked at the Abilene law offices of Col. E.C. Little and then as stenographer for the Dunlap Land Company. Moving to Missouri, she was a district court stenographer in Saline County, Missouri, where her stenography skills were praised in a 1909 Marshall Daily Democrat News following a murder trial. [cxxxii]

John Gofero was charged with killing John Spangler May 21, 1909, in Marshall. As the stenographer for Barbee & Roberts:

> Hershey *"exhibited the greatest skill in taking down evidence of the witnesses that testified, that ever was performed in this city. In fact, she equaled the record made by expert stenographers and typewriters at their annual conventions by writing and averaging throughout each day 15 pages of legal matter per hour, or 4,500 to 5, 000 words each hour. In addition to this, Miss Hershey had to take time to put in a carbon to make an extra copy, which required time in addition to her typewriting. At the end of the entire preliminary, Miss Hershey had written over 200 pages and seemed to be as fresh and ready for work as when she started."* [cxxxiii]

Soon after that, at age 23, Hershey entered the Lawrence (Kansas) Business College "with a determination to prepare herself for a good position as a stenographer." [cxxxiv] Of her school work, the Lawrence Daily World said her "bookkeeping was always neat and especially accurate … (and) each day's stenographic work mastered that day." [cxxxv]

After graduation in May 1910, she was stenographer for the Wichita (Kansas) Wholesale Grocery. She also worked for a prominent law firm in Oklahoma, before arriving in Jefferson City in early 1913.

Hershey arrived in Jefferson City in 1913 as a stenographer for the State Insurance Department under Director Charles Revelle. [cxxxvi] She continued in that work until her appointment to the Red Cross.

The Jefferson City Democrat called her "one of the most competent stenographers in the state." [cxxxvii] Hershey won the Underwood Typewriter Company's national typewriting contest in October 1913, while already employed as a stenographer with the state insurance department, for the best essay on speed and accuracy in less than 125 words. [cxxxviii]

Her fiancé, Thorpe Gordon, was four years her junior, born in 1891 near Scruggs Station. He had joined the Walther-Wymore Furniture and Undertaking Company, the first funeral home in Jefferson City, in 1910 and was a licensed embalmer. [cxxxix cxl]

Gordon was a non-commissioned officer with the 337th Machine Gun Battalion 88th Division. He departed Aug. 15, 1918, from Brooklyn, New York. [cxli] After arriving "somewhere in England," he wrote home Sept. 1, 1918, that all was well and he was impressed with England.

Hershey also felt it was "her patriotic duty to do what she can to help win the war" by volunteering with the American Red Cross, the Abilene Weekly Reflector said. [cxlii]

Her assignment, which came with a significant reduction in salary, was to be a stenographer for the aid organization in Switzerland. [cxliii] After visiting her family in Abilene, Kansas, she boarded a ship bound for France just weeks after her fiancé and only a month before the war's end.

But she died of pneumonia aboard the transport ship and was buried at sea. [cxliv]

Although her mother, Jennie, had received word Oct. 22, 1918, of Hershey's safe arrival in France, the information was incorrect. [cxlv] Again, her family received a communication error, when a cable arrived from Paris Oct. 30, 1918, saying "Winifred Heath" had been buried at sea. They had to telegraph Washington D.C. for an explanation, which is when they learned it was Hershey who had been buried at sea. [cxlvi] They received no explanation for the safe arrival telegram the week before.

The director of the American Red Cross, W.R. Castle, sent a letter to her mother that was published in the Abilene newspaper:

"I hope that you will remember always that she as truly died in the service of this

country and this civilization as if she had been a soldier killed by the Germans in the frontline trenches. Miss Hershey was on a mission to help the U.S. win this war by merciful assistance to the soldiers of the country. Her mission was doubly important for this reason and you must always think of her as a crusader who gave her life before she could accomplish her high purpose." [cxlvii] – W.R. Castle

The American Red Cross still was a small organization, growing and developing its identity, when Europe was thrown into conflict in 1914. Aid workers began serving immediately, though the U.S. did not declare war on Germany until April 1917. And their work continued for three years after the war ended in November 1918. During that seven-year period, Hershey was one of 400 American Red Cross workers who died, including 296 women. [cxlviii]

Grace Hershey

She is the only woman listed among Cole County's World War I casualties on the monument at the Cole County Courthouse, 301 E. High St. A bronze eagle sits atop the monument provided by collaboration of state appropriation, interest from a memorial fund, the county government, the Rotary Club and women's clubs. The rough granite obelisk, which symbolizes "sturdy character and steadfastness of American troops," Jeremy Amick wrote in "Jefferson City at War: 1916-1975." The St. Louis Brass Company cast the bronze memorial tablet listing the names of 57 men and Hershey: "In Memory of the men from Cole County who died in the service of their state and Country in the World's War 1917 to 1918." [cxlix]

In her hometown, the Ladies of the Presbyterian Church donated to equip a patient room in her honor at the 1922-built Dickinson County Memorial Hospital. [cl] Her name also is on a bronze plate of gold stars at the hospital, naming 51 soldiers, sailors, marines and nurses from the county who died in service during World War I. [cli]

Nationally, Hershey is among 161 women on the Women's Overseas Service League's Gold Star Women list, compiled for Armistice Day 1922 to recognize "American girls who gave their lives in the world war." [clii] She was the only one from Kansas. Most were buried in France, but others were in Siberia, Armenia, China, Manila and England. Four other women from Missouri are remembered – Katherine Hoffman, Queen City; Catherine Cecil, St. Louis; Margaret Keirn, Schlater; and Ina Klinfelter, Diamond. [cliii]

She was "a bright and interesting young woman of much personal charm, loyal to friends and pleasant and kind to everyone," the Hope

(Kansas) Dispatch said Nov. 7, 1918. In death, she "will come forth as one of the heroines in the cause of humanity and righteousness." [cliv]

6 EMMA COLGAN SANFORD MATHEWS
Frontier Woman Made a Home for Others

- ❖ Born: March 17, 1820, St. Charles County, Missouri
- ❖ Death: Oct. 10, 1886, Jefferson City, Missouri
- ❖ Notable: Among the earliest female business owners in the Capital City

Life on the frontier of Missouri was rugged and unpredictable. Emma Colgan was born into one of the earliest families to settle in Mid-Missouri. She knew the vulnerability of living in the virgin woods with threats of attack from the native people. She knew the hardships of trading goods along the Missouri River with nothing but a flatboat to make its way down the muddy water. And she knew the necessity of perseverance, regardless of loss or loneliness.

Born in the spring of 1820, her parents were Robert Colgan Sr. and Maria Rogers. She was the oldest of three children born in St. Clair, Franklin County. [clv] Her grandfather, Daniel Colgan Sr., was born in Delaware before the Revolutionary War and reared his family in Berkeley County, Virginia, until relocating to Jefferson County, Kentucky, in 1788. [clvi] Daniel Colgan Sr. farmed and ran a sizeable tailoring business in Shelbyville, Kentucky, until 1806.

The Colgan family arrived in the new Louisiana Purchase territory in late 1806, building a log cabin (where the county poor house was in 1876) on a 500-acre farm in rural St. Charles County. [clvii] He built a trap door under his cabin, which he opened each night so that the native people entered his home, they would fall into the cellar. But, his home was never attacked. [clviii]

In 1812, when Emma's father was 25, the Colgan family moved to the city of St. Charles, where he opened a tailor's shop, dressing deer skins and making pants and hunting shirts. According to "A History of the Pioneer Families of Missouri," Emma's grandfather kept a pet bear, which once broke its chain to chase boys who had been tormenting it. [clix]

By 1817, the Colgan family set up trade at Cote sans Dessein, Callaway

County. While the patriarch remained in St. Charles, Emma's father, Bob, along with his brothers Daniel and Harvey, were among the sparse residents at the largest settlement west of St. Louis at the time. [clx] Harvey Colgan, a contractor, built the second Missouri Executive Mansion and what is known today at Lohman's Landing. [clxi]

At this original French trapper settlement, Bob Colgan brought his wife Maria Rogers. She had been born in Missouri territory with French heritage. As a child, Maria had helped her parents defend their home on the Gasconade River when native people attacked them, by loading the guns for her father. [clxii]

Emma Colgan spent the first five or so years of her life at the river settlement, before her parents returned to St. Clair, where her twin brothers, Nicholas and Robert Jr. were born in 1826.

At age 25, Emma Colgan married Lt. Col. Alfred Sanford in 1845 in St. Louis. Sanford was born in 1788 in Westmoreland, Virginia, making him 38 years her senior, or the same age as her father. During the War of 1812, he served as adjutant of J.M. Scott's Regiment of the Kentucky Volunteers. [clxiii]

Sanford was orphaned by age 20 in Campbell County, Kentucky. There, he married Susan Lewis Martin, with whom he had eight children between 1814 and 1832, when she died in childbirth. His oldest daughter, Indiana, married Col. Daniel Whiting in 1834. When Sanford moved to St. Louis, before 1840, he left his children with Indiana.

Four years after Emma married Sanford, his daughter, Indiana, also died in childbirth. His second youngest daughter, Scioto, married that same year, 1849, Maj. Richard Gatlin, and moved to Arkansas. By 1851, the Gatlins were living in St. Louis. After Scioto died a week after childbirth, Emma and Sanford likely took in Scioto's older son, John, who died at age 4 in 1854 in St. Louis. [clxiv]

The Sanfords moved to Jefferson City some time after that. At age 73, Sanford was a gardener in 1860. Sanford's youngest daughter, Orphena, and her daughter, Susan Lawrence, 8, were living with them. After Sanford died in 1863, Orphena moved to Washington D.C. and lived with her surrogate father/brother-in-law Daniel Whiting. [clxv]

In August 1865, Emma Sanford leased, remodeled and newly-furnished the Capitol House, 101 Washington St., with "particular attention to accommodate members of the General Assembly (since it) is much nearer the Capitol building than any other boarding house in the city," the Missouri State Times said. [clxvi]

Two years later, she took over the American House, opposite the Pacific Railroad depot. [clxvii]

With personal estate valued at $3,500 (about $70,000 today), Emma was keeping house with two domestic servants and a porter living with her in 1870. By February 1871, she operated "Ladies and Gents' Restaurant and

Day Board" on High Street, near Riddler's Drug Store. [clxviii]

Emma had returned to the Capitol House in May 1874 as a co-owner with M.E. Eiker and L.W. Painter. [clxix] After refitting and furnishing the "comfortable and pleasant rooms," Emma was sole owner within seven months. [clxx] Local doctor A.M. Davison had bought the property from George B. Ransome in 1873 and improved the property, just across from the second Capitol, from 20 to 33 "good-sized rooms". [clxxi]

For a time, she also served as matron at the Missouri State Penitentiary. [clxxii]

Mrs. Emma Sanford was "well and favorably known to citizens and the traveling public (as an) amiable hostess of the Capitol House," when she leased the Tennessee House in September 1875. "She knows how to keep a hotel (and is) worthy and deserving," the People's Tribune said. "The reputation of the Tennessee House will be well-sustained by Mrs. Sanford." [clxxiii]

From The People's Tribune Feb. 8, 1871

From The State Journal April 2, 1875

The property owner, Tennessee Mathews, had closed the 18-year-old public hotel "having neither time to spare, nor money to squander, in testing the constitutionality of congressional informies," he said in a March 1875 notice in the People's Tribune. However, he continued the private boarding for select guests. [clxxiv]

The Tennessee House was built by 1857 on the south side of the 100 block of East High Street with 47 guest rooms. [clxxv]

In June 1859, the hotel was again under Dr. Mathews' operation. He enlarged and improved the facilities with new furniture, including bed and bedding. [clxxvi]

The three-story, frame building offered room on its main floor for retail, such as Sachs and Wolferman Dry Goods and Clothing, the People's Tribune business office, his son's law offices, J.T. Craven Shoe Store, and the W.M. and S.H. Sone Jr. stagecoach office. [clxxvii]

In March 1863, Mathews added a large brick addition, to accommodate an additional 100 guests. C.P. Anderson, editor of the Weekly California

News at the time, said he "knows how to keep a hotel and the numerous guests, members of the legislature and others seemed to feel perfectly at home." [clxxviii]

The Tennessee House was praised for its large, airy rooms and its sense of home. "The doctor himself is one of nature's noblemen, true type of an old-time gentleman, companionable and pleasant in his intercourse, sympathetic in his nature and courteous and polite to every one," the California Democrat reported in February 1874. At that time, his wife of 16 years, Henriette, and daughter, Roxanne, were involved in the management.

Mathews, a doctor and druggist by training, opened his practice in Jefferson City about 1844. [clxxix] He graduated from Louisville Medical College in 1842 and arrived in time to treat victims of a series of cholera outbreaks in his first few years. After treating so many soldiers' wounds during the Civil War, Mathews gave up most of his medical practice, turning mostly to his drug store – The City Drug Store, opened in 1844.

Born in Dixon's Springs, Tennessee, his grandfather served with Gen. George Washington during the Revolutionary War and his father with Gen. Andrew Jackson in the War of 1812. [clxxx] He had three children from his first wife, though they all preceded him in death.

Mathews was known as "a peculiar man and a useful, and in many respects, original and honored citizen," his obituary said. He was known to dress in the Pickwickian style with a swallow tail coat, high collar, brass buttons and a large bow tie. [clxxxi]

He held broad and liberal views on many subjects and donated thousands of dollars to charitable activities. [clxxxii]

He also served as alderman and mayor, the prison doctor, county coroner and president of the fire department. He was a pioneer of Temperance and a member of the Independent Order of Good Templars, Capital City Lodge #111. [clxxxiii]

James Ford described Mathews as austere and unapproachable in appearance, but actually kind and warm-hearted. On several occasions, Mathews was called on by the community to help de-escalate situations. For example, during a riot in the Missouri State Penitentiary in the 1870s, the warden opposed bloodshed and wouldn't let the militia through. Yet, the city was panic stricken, so Mathews grabbed a gun, walked to the front of the militia and demanded the gates be opened. The rioters were surprised and quickly subdued. [clxxxiv]

Nine years after Emma Colgan Sanford took over operations of the Tennessee House, she married property owner Dr. Mathews. He was 77 and she was 65, married by the Rev. T.M. Cobb, pastor of the Methodist Episcopal Church South in front of many friends who gave them valuable presents. [clxxxv]

Emma kept her property separate from her second husband's, though she did keep proof and bonds in his safe. When she made her will in June 1886, she had $300 bonds in Butler County and $1,100 bonds in Lafayette County, as well as $560 – all of which she left to her cousins James Colgan, Ruth Colgan and Mary Mnefee. [clxxxvi] She preceded Mathews in death by four months.

The old Tennessee House was demolished in June 1899 by Schwartz and Brown. [clxxxvii] George Porth, a jeweler who moved to Jefferson City in 1879, bought the lots and built a three-story, red brick building in its place at 110-112-114 E. High St. [clxxxviii]

7 LYDIA ANNA GAYLORD HESS MONTAGUE

Abolitionist Teacher Broke Missouri Law to Open First Classroom for Jefferson City African Americans

"Whoever teaches in this city must need have a brave heart."

– Lydia Gaylord Hess Montague

❖ Born: June 14, 1817, Plymouth, Connecticut
❖ Died: Sept. 26, 1886, Carthage, Missouri
❖ Notable: First teacher of black students in Jefferson City

In June 1864, Jefferson City may have been occupied by Union soldiers, but the southern-leanings of the original pioneer families were still strongly evident. Many of the city's leaders were pro-Union but also pro-slavery.

Since 1847, teaching an African-American, free or slave, to read and write had been outlawed. And the January 1863 U.S. Emancipation Proclamation did not apply to those enslaved in Missouri, which remained loyal to the Union.

In these circumstances, Lydia Gaylord Hess Montague arrived, assigned by the American Missionary Association to open a school to educate black residents, like 13-year-old Josephine Jones Bennett, later the wife of 65th USCT veteran William Logan Bennett. [clxxxix]

After opening in June 1864 in a barn on the south end of the city, the unpopular mission school had several locations, including a "shack on Hobo Hill," where Lincoln Institute would open its first classes two years later. That is where, Bennett, the daughter of a cabinet maker living at 514 Monroe St., remembered being taught by Montague. [cxc]

The 47-year-old widow twice over had worked with her oldest daughter, Lydia Hess, with freedmen in St. Louis and her younger daughter, Dantie, was teaching similarly in Alton, Illinois. At the same time, all three of her sons and her husband had served in the Union army, two of her sons being wounded and her husband having died.

In August 1862, early reports said her son Byron, who was a first sergeant with the 3rd Michigan Infantry, was killed at the second Battle of Bull Run. Instead, he had been shot twice in the left arm. While visiting his mother in December 1862, his arm was amputated. But, he was commissioned into the Veterans Reserve Corps in March 1864 in Philadelphia. [cxci]

Oliver, her son, was wounded three times and discharged from the 8th Illinois Cavalry. He served at the sieges of Richmond, Gaines' Mill and Antietam and was the first to ford the Rappahannock at Fredericksburg. And, her third son, Henry served with the 1st Iowa Cavalry.

So, the cause was important to her entire family.

An easterner born in Connecticut and reared in New York, Montague moved in 1837 with her first husband, Diocletian Hess, and their oldest two sons to Michigan, where she gave birth to their third under a tent of quilts soon after arriving. She and Hess were instrumental in starting the first Methodist Sabbath school in their area. After Hess died at age 42, she married William Montague in 1855.

When the war began, Lydia Montague was left on their Michigan family farm before joining her daughter, Lydia Hess, who also had taught in Michigan, in St. Louis.

Lydia Hess was known as a "thorough, practical teacher" and arrived in April 1863 in St. Louis to assist J.L. Richardson at the Missouri Hotel to help teach freedmen. [cxcii] The school moved to the Ebenezer Church on Washington Avenue, St. Louis, in May, but the building was burned after two days of classes. [cxciii] Then, they returned to the hotel with an average daily attendance of 100. [cxciv]

In the fall of 1863, Hess helped open the American Free School on Seventh Street, St. Louis. [cxcv] She was in charge of the school's full operation by early 1864, seeing an average of 100 students, mostly former slaves arrived from other states. Hess observed in St. Louis that locals "spurn the idea of sending their children to the same school with these poor children" newly-arrived from southern states. [cxcvi]

Of her students, Hess said they were "generally quick to learn, the secret is perhaps, their great anxiety to know how to read." [cxcvii]

After Montague joined her daughter at the St. Louis school in January 1864, she said: "I am really interested in the work you have assigned us. I was always an abolitionist in sentiment, yet in becoming acquainted with the colored people I am happily disappointed, finding them as easy to learn and as capable of attainments as the general class of white people." [cxcviii]

Mr. Early, the presiding elder of one of the African-American churches in Jefferson City, visited Hess in April 1864 in St. Louis. The association had promised to send a teacher to Jefferson City some months before. And without result, Early was on his way to Philadelphia, Pennsylvania, to recruit an alternate teacher. He told Hess "he had lost confidence in the American Missionary Association for their delay and had intended to look for a teacher from some other source." [cxcix]

"I have felt deeply the importance of a good school at that point, one that could claim the protection of the military authority and a school taught by a colored teacher might fail in awakening their sympathy," Montague wrote. [cc] And so, Montague was assigned to open the American Missionary Association's first work in Jefferson City. [cci]

The Free Colored School opened June 13, 1864, in a log barn on what was then called Thomas Street, in the south part of the city. [ccii] On her first day, Montague met 60 students and a week later, 80 were in attendance. [cciii] It was a log school house, "entirely too small but much better than none." [cciv] So many students turned out that they "often spilled out into the dusty streets during lessons." [ccv]

Students walked up to two miles and working men were eager for a night school. [ccvi] "Some ... were still slaves. Their masters permitted them to attend classes when they completed their work for the day." [ccvii]

"The prospects of the school is much favorable. This is the first effort of the kind here and the colored people are so very grateful," Montague wrote. "They are but lately from slavery a number of them are slaves now." [ccviii]

A Union soldier helped her for a few sessions. And an African-American man helped her teach a Sabbath school to nearly 100. Later, she also received help from an eager young white boy for a time. [ccix] Montague said she had hoped some of the "radical" people in town would help her, too, but it "is not popular." [ccx]

"I am very sanguine in the belief that I can do away with the prejudice against 'educating niggers,' if I can have proper help," Montague said. "I want to make this a model school, if possible, so that it may gain the admiration of the legislature next winter." [ccxi]

After 37 sessions in 19 days, Montague had seen 154 different students with an average attendance of 80. More than 40 of her students were older than 16 and the gender break was three girls to every two boys. After that first month, 80 could write, 25 could read and spell and 25 were doing mental arithmetic. [ccxii]

"People that are friendly to the cause express astonishment that she has accomplished so much in so short a time. ... A number that at first did not know their letters are now reading and spelling," Montague's daughter said. [ccxiii]

Hess joined her mother in August 1864. The weather was "extremely warm" and the schoolhouse "very uncomfortable." And she found her mother "quite unwell, probably from being overworked." In a letter to Rev. Whipple, Lydia Hess wrote: "Her school besides being very large, required extra care to teach them what was required …" [ccxiv]

Eventually, Montague's other daughter, Diantha, was assigned to help her in Jefferson City. [ccxv] Montague and her daughters encountered local leaders opposed to her mission and most anti-slavery residents afraid to speak out. Her school was harrassed and she was turned away by any boarding options near her work.

"I was disappointed when I got here to find people mostly of strong 'secesh' principles," Montague wrote to the association's leader. "Had I known the state of things, I would have obtained an order from Gen. (William) Rosecrans before I left." [ccxvi]

"The prejudice is so strong against the 'nigger teacher.' I have since found quite a number of radicals, but they have to be very careful, as the commander of this district is 'cesh (as they say) and the mayor is still worse." [ccxvii] She found in the town "a great many slave-holding (residents) and opposed to the education of the colored race." [ccxviii]

Within her first two weeks, Montague feared she would have to abandon her school, due to the opposition. She referred to the rebels' influence as "venom," and, in general, described the place as "a poor county for anyone, and it is no place for the blacks." [ccxix] Even the occupying "military authority refused to protect it," without an order from Gen. Rosecrans, who was in command of the Department of Missouri at the time. [ccxx]

More than just words and sentiment, some residents in Jefferson City were active in their opposition to Montague's school. "The white boys have been very troublesome," she wrote after only 10 days in town. [ccxxi] Several white boys had entered her schoolhouse through the window and "endeavored to make a general wreck," destroying some of her few books, before they were discovered and run off. [ccxxii]

These white boys then focused their attention on the male students, throwing rocks at them as they approached and left the school. Eventually, the father of one of them discovered what they were doing and shamed them. [ccxxiii]

Montague did find some support, when a German justice called on her, saying he would protect the school if the black students would not retaliate and escalate the situation. [ccxxiv]

"Whoever teaches in this city must need have a brave heart," she said. [ccxxv]

Even the mayor and the militia commander were "copperheads." Mayor Matthew Martin Flesh, a German immigrant age 29, served one term in 1864. Montague said he "painted and raised the rebel flag in this city," which may be true, as his occupation was as a painter. [ccxxvi] And a local story says a rebel flag – composed of red and white stripes and 8 stars in an incomplete circle - was raised at the Basye House, at the southeast corner of Water and Madison streets, in May 1861 following the state convention's decision to remain loyal to the Union. [ccxxvii]

Mayor Flesh approached Montague on several occasions trying to strong-arm her into closing the school, saying "the thing must be stopped." [ccxxviii] She reported: "This interference of the mayor waked up some more radical friends who, being no friend of the mayor, immediately took sides in my favor of the school." [ccxxix]

Twice Flesh threatened legal action, as it was still technically illegal to teach African Americans. When Mayor Flesh asked Montague what authority she had to teach this school, her reply was she was "healing the laws of the state." [ccxxx]

R.J. Lackey, son-in-law of former Gov. Austin King and the district attorney general, came to her aid. "I had closed amid the fear in sobs of the children and thought best to give it up unless I would get the military protection," she said. [ccxxxi]

Lackey instructed Capt. Price to allow the school and that the mayor did not have authority to close it. "He said go on at all hazards and if they tried to drive us out, to hold our ground, stone them or take any course I thought best to protect the school and, if they offered me any violence, to shoot them," Montague reported. [ccxxxii]

Fortunately, the mayor left about that time, being connected with the army. And for the next two weeks, "our school has had a peaceful quiet." [ccxxxiii]

But then, former mayor Thomas Lawson Price took up the threats. [ccxxxiv]

Pierce Buffington, who was a man of influence and who had helped hundreds of former slaves, had a run-in with Price. The former mayor had been drinking and told Buffington that the colored school must be stopped and should be - in harsh language - denounced the idea of teaching niggers." Price further revealed a plot was in place to run them out soon. [ccxxxv]

Fortuitously, new Union troops arrived in the Capital City about that same time, as the Confederate raid of Gen. Sterling Price was headed north from Arkansas.

In July 1864, former and first Mayor Thomas Lawson Price held a large ball at his grand home at the southwest corner of Washington and High streets. In attendance were Gen. Egbert Brown, commander of the Central Missouri District; Col. Willard Hall, who also was lieutenant governor at the time; Gov. Hamilton Gamble and other men of a certain clique, Montague said. At that time, they divided into squads who began leaving the city after dark, headed south in the direction of a known rebel depot, she said. [ccxxxvi]

In August, about 200 guerillas came into the city. They killed one of the boarders at Montague's place and wounded another. Radicals of the city, including Buffington have been alert that summer. "Officers in power at Jefferson seem to be all copperheads," Montague observed. "The guerillas are trying to rid the state of every radical voter. In many instances they have scalped them after murdering them in the most savage manner." [ccxxxvii]

It reached the point that a raid in Jefferson City was expected daily. The African Americans were so frightened they would not come to school. And eventually, Montague, too, was scared enough to return to St. Louis Sept. 2, 1864.

In just the three months she was there, the school had been highly successful.

After leaving Jefferson City for St. Louis in September 1864, Montague attempted to revive the school at Benton Barracks, where enlisted black soldiers were mustered in. She also tried to get an order from Gen. Rosecrans to bring families of the soldiers from Jefferson City to the barracks. But Price's Raid in October 1864 prevented that. And then, the contraband lot was burned, making St. Louis no longer any better of a prospect for those families. ccxxxviii

Reflecting on her first year in the work of educating African Americans, Montague wrote to Rev. George Whipple: "This has been to me a work of deep interest, and I am truly thankful to God for giving me strength to be the means of aiding this unfortunate race in their initiatory experience in passing from the habits of slave life to that of freemen." ccxxxix

Montague and her youngest daughter, Dantie, then spent the fall of 1864 teaching in Alton, Illinois. But she continued to fret about her students and their families in Jefferson City and that she should have returned right away. ccxl

She decided to wait in St. Louis until the outcome of the Nov. 5, 1864, election, to determine whether the radicals would carry the state. If they hadn't, Montague anticipated the freedmen and women would have been returned to enslavement. ccxli

By December 1864, she was lobbying for the school in Jefferson City to resume and in January 1865, the African American community had written to her requesting her return. They said "there are many more colored people there than when I was there last summer and say they need two teachers now," Montague reported. ccxlii With the legislature back in session, "I think that the most important point now in Missouri," she said. ccxliii

Montague and Dantie returned to Jefferson City in early March 1865, after Gov. Thomas Fletcher had arranged for them to use the old Southern Methodist Church, on the south side of the 100 block of West Main Street, for the school house. However, by the time she arrived, the church had taken possession of their previously confiscated building. To prevent the black school from being located there, they had started a school with one teacher and four scholars there. ccxliv

She hoped to use Katsworth Hall, which the black Baptist church was trying to buy, but it was still occupied. Eventually, the log church where she had taught the previous summer was repaired and school resumed in late March 1865 with about 32 scholars. ccxlv

"I was very much disappointed when I came to find matters so unfavorable, but I have made the acquaintance of several state officers ... and they have guaranteed protection to me and the school," Montague wrote. ccxlvi

Still hoping for a larger schoolhouse, the school had to charge students 50-cents/month or $1/month for large families. But, that still would not cover the cost of board for two teachers. "The children all want to come to school, but their parents do not send the money and I do not like to turn them away," Montague said. Many mothers were alone, as their husbands were soldiers. ccxlvii

Bushwhackers were still a threat in the spring of 1865, taking out their spite on the freedmen, who "they shoot and hang without mercy. But, yet, they seem to be very cheerful and so thankful that they are free," Montague wrote. ccxlviii

As the Capital City, Montague believed it was "the most important place for a missionary school in Missouri. The appearance and credit of this school will have a great bearing on the action of the government and legislature," she wrote. ccxlix

In the meantime, the African American community was troubled by "a copperhead citizen who calls himself their friend," who interjected himself into their purchase of Katsworth Hall. Montague hired a lawyer to help sort it out. ccl In August 1865, her classes had moved into Katsworth Hall, which to someone wanting to be the African-American church's landlord at a sheriff's sale. ccli

When she arrived for school the next day, she found one of the African American Baptist deacons had locked the door and said she would have to pay 10 percent of the rent to the new owner. cclii Montague enlisted Nelson Burch, a lawyer and clerk of the Missouri Supreme Court, to draw up a lease agreement. ccliii That is when she learned from the deacon that their landlord warned the church trustees not to hold a school in their property until they paid off the property and then, the teacher should be one of their own race. ccliv

"This people in their transition from slavery to freedom hardly know what is for their own good but often take advice of their professed friends, who are leading them sadly astray," she wrote. cclv "It is this rebel in blue that has stopped the school. This Hubbard is hated by the radical party and they would like to ... expel him from the place." cclvi

State Treasurer William Bishop wrote a letter on her behalf to the Rev. George Whipple, one of the New York founders of the American Missionary Association in 1846. cclvii

"The self-sacrificing conduct of those ladies is worthy of all commendation. When they first established their school in this place, it was under the auspices of the military, though in direct violation of the statutory laws of this state. At that time, there were not more than half a dozen strictly loyal residents of this town, who sympathized with her and her mission for good. They were intimidated by the proslavery element by which they were surrounded," Bishop wrote. [cclviii]

"That which the rebels have failed to accomplish by force of arms, they now seek to accomplish by craft. In the states farther south, you know exactly the element with which you have to deal. Here it is different. Their course here is more covert and crafty, but not less bitter." [cclix]

Bishop referred to the purchase of the school to influence the black church to move out the school. Because the school is doing well, "this chagrins the old rebel element and they seek by craft to destroy it," he said. [cclx]

In addition to the white men fleecing the freedmen, the Methodist and Baptist congregations were contentious toward each other. Instead of working together, they each wanted their own school. [cclxi] And, their ministers were undermining each other. [cclxii]

Montague became discouraged, despite having her daughter, Dantie, there to help. They had neither received replies to her letters nor pay from the association. Yet, in May 1865, they averaged 100 students in school and 200 at Sabbath school. [cclxiii] Finally, in June 1865, she received $25, the first of any pay from the association since November 1864. [cclxiv]

"I have a laborious work and one very trying to one's nerves, my friends here say that I have the most moral courage of any woman they ever saw, but they little realize the heartaches, that I often feel, but do not think proper to express them," she wrote in May 1865. [cclxv] However, the "bitter prejudice against the education of the blacks is also, I think, wearing away." [cclxvi]

Montague extended her educational services from classroom and Sabbath into personal health, too. In August 1865, she reported many children were sick and dying. Visiting house to house, she was teaching parents how to nurse their children and which medicines to use, providing the medicine, when possible. [cclxvii]

"I feel that I am doing a great deal of good here and consequently am blessed in performing my duty," she said. [cclxviii]

Montague began night school in September 1865. "I feel that there is more need of a night school for the adults, both men and women, perhaps, than the days. There has been such bitter opposition ... (yet) they did progress, faster than any school I have ever taught among them." [cclxix]

In February 1866, Montague invited members of the General Assembly to attend one of the school's evening examinations. "They were highly gratified and some were really astonished, having thought it impossible for them to make such attainments," she wrote. "... We have spared no pains in trying to advance them, for I wished them to compete with the white school here." [cclxx]

Since Montague had arrived 20 months earlier, she had taught 300 people to read. And, at the Sabbath school, which still averaged 100 in attendance, she was preparing teachers from her day students. "I am so pleased with their improvement, that it does my heart good." [cclxxi]

The state school bill had just passed in February 1866, which gave her renewed hope to support the school for African Americans. However, the prejudice of the city was morphing into jealousy, she observed. The southern aristocratic families were frustrated by the improvements of the black men, Montague reported. [cclxxii]

All along, Montague struggled with finances. The African American community had little to contribute, especially when they also were trying to pay for their own church buildings. The American Missionary Association also was spread thin with its donations. She boarded cheaply and economized as best she could, even borrowing from her "crippled son," who had been wounded in the war. [cclxxiii]

In May 1866, Montague met Lt. Richard Baxter Foster, who sought her out. Foster was sent with the money and hopes of hundreds of soldiers from the 62nd and 65th U.S. Colored Troops, to establish a school for African Americans. After finding little prospects in St. Louis, Foster chose to open the school in the state Capitol. "I hope he may proceed in establishing such a school and that radical officers of the state wish to have it located here at Jefferson." [cclxxiv]

A month later, Lincoln Institute was formalized, under a board of trustees. "It is just what is needed," Montague wrote. "Heretofore, I have had not one to act with us and ... now we all feel so encouraged. May God bless and preserve the effort." [cclxxv]

Lincoln Institute opened in September 1866 in the "House on Hobo Hill," the dilapidated two-room cabin on Jackson Street, where Simonsen School is today, where Montague's school previously had met. The two schools existed simultaneously for more than a year.

Montague returned to St. Louis to help her, Lydia, in late 1867, leaving the Jefferson City school under charge of Diantha, assisted by Esther Ann Buffington, a graduate of the Pennsylvania Female College. [cclxxvi]

Quakers from Chester County, Pennsylvania, the Buffingtons arrived in Missouri with their abolitionist views about 1857. [cclxxvii] Even after their home was robbed, the family continued to aid the freedmen. They were a great support to Montague in a town of opposition or silent support. "Had it not been for the sympathy and aid of that family, I fear the school at Jefferson would have languished," she said. [cclxxviii]

Montague endorsed Esther Buffington as young, active and "one of the noblest specimens of womanhood, ... (who) had for some time wished to engage in some philanthropic work but had been detained by the care of her father's family." [cclxxix]

The former had hoped the latter would continue the school after

Diantha Hess married Peter Hill in November 1867 and moved to Carthage. [cclxxx] However, Buffington was replaced by a stranger sent by the association.

Of these women and their early mission, Lt. Foster, as the first teacher and principal at Lincoln Institute, said: They had "done an immense work in transforming the freedmen into free men; in loosing the bonds of ignorance, when the government had loosed the bonds of slavery. It was their fate, as it has been for thousands before and will be of thousands to come, to sow in tears, but not to reap in joy, to lay foundations on which others should build." [cclxxxi]

Montague continued to keep up with the progress of the mission school at Jefferson City until it closed in 1868. [cclxxxii]

She saw the school progress from a small log barn, so crowded there wasn't room for writing desks, to the Baptist church hall. Hundreds of faces came and went, learning what had been illegal from Montague and her daughter.

Montague boarded great distance and as an older woman, suffered from the heat, long hours, indignation of months without pay and the general stress of the situation. Yet she persevered. Her great mission was to help the newly-freed men and women improve themselves for independence.

"My sole object is to benefit this race, while I am with them," she wrote. [cclxxxiii] "In all the places where I have been acquainted, I have never had my sympathies called out for them, as here." [cclxxxiv]

Although she left the Jefferson City school in 1867, Montague continued to assist her daughter, Lydia, teaching at schools for African Americans in St. Louis. As late as 1879, she was teaching at Sumner High School. [cclxxxv]

Her children were successful, too. Byron and Oliver both moved to St. Louis after the war to study at St. Louis Medical College and Washington University law school, respectively. Byron had a practice and drugstore in their hometown in Michigan. Oliver's law practice included a run for governor of Colorado. And Henry was a dentist in Colorado.

Montague is buried in Carthage, as she died in 1886 while visiting her children, Diantha and Oliver.

8 ESTELLA BRANHAM DIGGS
Strengthened by Faith, Driven by Compassion

❖ Born: Aug. 31, 1872, Jefferson City, Missouri
❖ Death: Oct. 16, 1970, Jefferson City, Missouri
❖ Notable: Musician, missionary, socialite, civil rights leader

Although she did not rear her own children, Estella F. Branham Diggs planted seeds of opportunity and nurtured cooperation between the races, which has benefited generations.

A strong woman of faith, she began teaching Sunday School at Second Baptist Church as a teenager, soon after her personal conversion experience. Devoted to that church, she gave decades of service as musician, teacher and representative to the greater Baptist community. She even donated property, when the church was in need of a new parsonage.

She was well-educated and intensely involved in community betterment. She led fraternal organizations, women's clubs, and charitable collection drives. Diggs also was instrumental in the creation and operation of the Jefferson City Community Center. And, she served on the earliest city-wide race relations committees.

In addition to these many contributions, Diggs was helpmate to one of the African-American community's business leaders, John "Duke" Diggs. And she has the distinguishment of being the first black woman to represent the 2nd Congressional District Republican party as a presidential elector..

Diggs was born in 1872 to George W. Branham and Frances "Fannie" Arnold. [cclxxxvi] She grew up at 213 Dunklin St., the second of seven children.

Her father was born a slave to the Andrew Branham family, which owned a farm near Bloomfield in Callaway County. He enlisted with the 4th Missouri Volunteers of African Descent, which became the 68th U.S.

Colored Troops, in March 1864. For a time, he was the regimental butcher before mustering out in February 1866 at Camp Parapet, Louisiana. [cclxxxvii] Two brothers also served - Robert joined the 68th U.S.C.T and Jerry the 56th U.S.C.T. [cclxxxviii]

Branham married Fannie Arnold in August 1866, soon after returning home. He supported his family as a laborer and plasterer. [cclxxxix]

Estella's paternal grandmother, America, had seven children with her first husband, John Ransom, who was enslaved by the Ransom family, who lived on Cedar Creek in Callaway County, but was hired out to work on Chafee's woodyard. America was enslaved by Martin Herndon Branham, also in Callaway County. The couple were together 12 years, until about 1856 when Ransom was sold to a Mr. Huffington, who moved away. [ccxc] Estella's father, George, was 11 at the time and recalled his father "was taken away by the white people and taken up into the country; I never saw him anymore." [ccxci]

Estella's mother, Fannie, was born into slavery but somewhere "south of the Mason Dixon line." Intelligent and attractive, she grew up in Boone County, the favorite of her owners, receiving kindness and comfort. She ate her meals with the family in the dining room, slept at the foot of her mistress' bed, and wore her mistress' old clothes. At age 14, she was left alone with her master, who made advances. She fled the home and ran to a toll gate, where the ferry owner stayed near the bridge to help other runaway slaves. At age 16, she moved to Jefferson City. [ccxcii]

Fannie was a founding member of Second Baptist Church and was the oldest member of the church at her death at age 99 in 1949. [ccxciii] After Estella's father's died in 1903, Fannie worked as a pastry cook at a local hotel, likely the Madison House, where Estella's brother Sanders was a waiter. [ccxciv]

The church became an early conduit for Estella's talents of teaching, leading and musicianship. She was baptized at age 13 and immediately took up duties as a Sunday school teacher and organist. [ccxcv] Diggs also organized the Young Women's Circle at Second Baptist Church, serving more than a decade as president. It later was named in her honor. [ccxcvi]

When Second Baptist installed a new Hammond organ in 1953, Diggs already had served 40 years as church musician. She had the honor of unveiling the organ, prior to recitals by Lincoln's Dr. O.A. Fuller and A. Lawrence Kimbrough. [ccxcvii]

And, in 1970, when the church razed its parsonage as well as its 1894-church building at 501 Monroe St. to build its present facility, Diggs donated one of her properties at 220 E. Ashley St. to replace the parsonage for the Rev. Harreld N. Nance. "We didn't know where we were going to get the money for a new parsonage," Nance said. [ccxcviii]

Diggs' involvement in church activities beyond the local congregation began at age 14, when she was elected corresponding secretary of the Central District Baptist Association of Missouri and, later she was elected corresponding secretary of the Baptist Mission Circle Central District Association. ccxcix

She was a long-time advocate of missions.

Diggs was active in the Missouri Baptist Women's Missionary Union (WMU) and the World Baptist Alliance. She represented Second Baptist at national and international conventions throughout the 1930s and 1940s, visiting New York City, Atlanta, Georgia and Copenhagen, Denmark, among others. ccc

One of the key roles she took on was improving interracial relations within the Baptist convention. In 1945, she was chairman of the Interracial Relations Committee of the Missouri Baptist Convention. ccci And in 1949, she was a featured speaker at the first of a series of five state interracial conferences, sponsored by the Baptist WMU and held in Kansas City. cccii In 1950, she was a speaker and leader in the regional interracial institutes, serving as vice president and delivering the key not message at the convention. ccciii

Diggs traveled to Copenhagen, Denmark, in July 1947 – when domestic

Courtesy Missouri State Archives Duke Diggs Collection

travel for Black citizens was treacherous - as one of 5,000 delegates to the World Baptist Alliance. ccciv Afterward, she toured seven other countries, including the devastated lands of Europe and the Holy Land, returning in October with souvenirs from the Sea of Galilee; the Dead Sea; Genoa, Italy; Palestine; Amsterdam, Holland; and Grasse, France. cccv

"The group with whom she traveled experienced no segregation and had a most enjoyable trip," the Clarion reported. "The new Jerusalem is beautiful and modernistic, in contrast to the old Bible days." cccvi

At home, Diggs earned a bachelor's degree and taught school at Olean, before marrying Duke Diggs in 1893. After his death in 1943, she finished her Master of Arts degree at Western Baptist Seminary.

Duke Diggs supported his wife as a cook, and later as a popular caterer, for the first few years, before opening his own transport business, moving furniture and other goods with horse and wagon. As he became a well-known and respected businessman, his company flourished and evolved into trucking. [cccvii]

The prosperous couple bought land and built a home at 526 Lafayette St. about 1918. [cccviii] Together, the Diggs were active in civic issues, as well as statewide politics, advocating to the General Assembly for African-American rights and for Lincoln University. [cccix]

Estella and Duke Diggs were both active in the United Brothers of Friendship and the Sisters of the Mysterious 10, at one time the "largest negro secret organization in the state." [cccx] The former organization was established in 1861 by freedmen and slaves in Kentucky, as a benevolent association to care for the sick and bury the dead. [cccxi] It spread to neighboring states by 1875. The Sisters of Friendship was the auxiliary until 1918, when the Sisters of the Mysterious Ten was formed. [cccxii]

As early as 1907, Estella was among the state organization's leaders, serving as the Grand Senior Marshal. [cccxiii] The fraternal organization's state convention was held in Jefferson City in 1910. Gov. Herbert Hadley and Mayor John F. Heinrichs greeted the more than 700 delegates gathered for four days. Estella Diggs and Lincoln University professor John Wesley Damel delivered greetings from the local lodges. [cccxiv] She was among eight convention speakers in 1921 and was named Grand Princess of the Sisters in 1934. [cccxv]

Duke Diggs served as Grand Secretary 1918-1934. [cccxvi]

The couple may best be remembered for their work to develop the Jefferson City Community Center.

"The Community Center was her idea and the construction of it was her passion, to give those in the black community a place to congregate, to learn and help others," said niece Sylvia Morris Ferguson.[cccxvii]

Estella was a founding member in 1906 of the Modern Priscilla Art and Charity Club – later renamed the Estella Branham Diggs Circle, which formed the Jefferson City Community Center Association in 1935. [cccxviii] The purpose was "to serve the Negro citizens of Jefferson City in the matter of welfare, reconstruction, education, charity, recreation, social life and other matters conducive to good citizenship." [cccxix]

The Modern Priscilla club's motto was "life is too short to waste." When the Community Chest was formed in 1925 to combine fundraising for local benevolent organizations, the Modern Priscillas were among the original nine organizations. They helped where they could until the Depression hit. Then, the club increased its work through a small building at 608 Dunklin St., where it stored and distributed commodities.

Looking next to provide hot lunches for school children, the community center idea was born. The first expansion was a partnership with the local Lions Clubs to create a chaperoned neighborhood park. Then, a second building on Dunklin Street expanded social services and offered a day nursery for children of working mothers.

In 1942, the community center association was ready to build the present stone building and received community-wide support. Although in failing health, Duke Diggs directed the construction project from his bed. And the entryway was named in his honor. Estella Diggs was the association's recording secretary for decades from its beginning. cccxx

In 1949, Estella Diggs was among the original members appointed by Mayor Lawrence Lutkewitte to the city's first-ever racial relations committee. Other members were Dr. Sidney J Reedy, Ruth Hardiman, Mary Brooks, A.L. Crow, Rev. John Maguire, Charles E. Robinson, Dr. Sherman Scruggs, Dr. A.S. Pride, Mrs. Julius Meyerhardt and Rev. Ned Cole. The commission's "overall purpose the promotion of good relations between all the citizens of our city, regardless of race, creed, color or national origin." cccxxi The major success of this short-lived racial relations commission was the integration of the armed forces service center.

However, it also promoted awareness of issues. For example, during the National Brotherhood Week of 1951, the commission announced a six-goal program to promote race relations. The issues address included educational and employment opportunities, integration of recreational facilities, opportunities to develop family and spiritual life, improved living facilities and a representative government. cccxxii

The next year, the city's Commission on Human Relations was created with many members from the previous committee included, including Estella Diggs. New members were Chairman Malcolm B. Epstien, Rev. Henry J Damm, Wilbur Kirkpatrick, Rev. Fr. John McGuire, and Lincoln librarian A.P. Marshall. cccxxiii

"It may seem strange that Jefferson City has suddenly made a turn for better brotherhood, but the facts show that this same turn is being made throughout the nation. Americans have finally awakened to the fact that one can't preach democracy abroad and not practice it at home," The Clarion May 2, 1952, edition said. cccxxiv

This was not her first taste of politics. In 1944, she became the first African-American woman to represent the 2nd Congressional District Republicans as a presidential elector to the Republican National Convention. cccxxv She was not among the original delegates nominated. However, Houston Ellis of Bunceton protested that the delegation included no African Americans. cccxxvi

The district's custom had been to elect an African American as an alternate delegate each year. This time, a black man from Jefferson City,

R.W. Stokes, was defeated for alternate. Instead, two white women were named as alternates. [cccxxvii]

Ellis' concern was that the party was losing its African American members. He lept to his feet and shouted: "We're getting no consideration whatever." [cccxxviii]

"I'm not pleading here for social equality," Ellis declared. "What do we care about eating at the same table with you or marrying white women?" "Just give the Negro race some representation so we can go out over the state to campaign and tell our people they are not forgotten by the party which freed them from slavery." [cccxxix]

Until her death in 1970, Diggs continued to work for her faith and community betterment, such as helping organize a youth division of the NAACP, focusing on Lincoln University students. [cccxxx] She also managed several real estate holdings, designed and built by her husband.[cccxxxi]

She suffered from osteoporosis, which eventually kept her in a wheelchair.[cccxxxii] But she continued to teach and play music on a grand piano at her 711 Jackson St. home, built with her mobility in mind.[cccxxxiii] At 224 E. Dunklin St., Diggs had built another home for her sisters, Theresa and Georgia.[cccxxxiv]

"Estella Diggs is one of the busiest of our first citizens in Jefferson City. To sum it all up she is always in the front rank of every progressive venture and project established fundamentally for the greatest good to the largest number," a 1945 Lincoln University Clarion article said. [cccxxxv]

9 JERENA EAST GIFFEN
She Made History, then she Preserved it

- ❖ Born: Nov. 15, 1924, Newcastle, Wyoming
- ❖ Died: Nov. 2, 2016, Danvers, Massachusetts
- ❖ Notable: First female bureau chief for United Press Inc.

When the Missouri State Prison lit up with riot fires Sept. 24, 1954, Jerena East was dressed for dinner with her fiancé at the Steamboat Lounge inside the Missouri Hotel. [cccxxxvi] Her future husband, Larry Giffen, was left on his own, when word reached her of one of the biggest events in Jefferson City's history.

"At the time, Jefferson City Capitol reporters were familiar with the tension at the prison. We had a standing joke in the press room at the Capitol that we had to drop coverage of the legislature because there was a riot at the prison. When I received a call telling me there was a riot, I had to be told several times by a fellow reporter that it was no joke," Giffen. "I went to the prison as fast as I could and was there for several hours. I finally remembered I had forgotten to call Larry." [cccxxxvii]

In heels, nylons and an evening dress, she was the only female reporter on the scene and likely was the best dressed. As Bureau Chief in the Capital City for United Press Inc., just nine month earlier, East had been at the prison for another national news event – the dual execution of child kidnapper-murderers Carl Austin Hall and Bonnie Brown Heady. [cccxxxviii]

On this night, inmates burned eight buildings and caused more than $5 million in damages. Of the 3,200 inmates at what was one of the largest prisons in the nation at the time, 30 prisoners and three guards were injured and four inmates died. It took the assistance of more than 1,000 policemen, Missouri National Guard, Missouri Highway Patrol and American Legion to quell the inside and outside of the walls. [cccxxxix]

East arrived at the prison administration building to find Gov. Phil

Donnelly, who told her it was too dangerous to allow reporters inside. However, she and a few other reporters managed their way in, anyway. [cccxl]

"It was mass confusion inside and out, as injured inmates were carried to offices, away from further danger. ... East stepped outside once for fresh air and found it almost as chaotic outside," Mark Schreiber wrote in "Somewhere In Time." [cccxli]

Her fiancé wanted to see the excitement, so East told Giffen to grab a camera and pose as a news photographer. "He got in the prison and took a great picture of a blood-soaked stretcher propped against the wall," East said. [cccxlii]

A few days later, East and Associated Press reporter George Sitterley hesitated to attend a University of Missouri-Columbia football game, which took them 30 miles from the smoldering scene. They compromised by keeping an eye on the Missouri Highway Patrol superintendent Col. Hugh Waggoner. When he suddenly got up to leave the game, they followed him and found out, sure enough, there was trouble at the prison again. [cccxliii]

"My car was blocked by the football parking set up and I couldn't get out," East recalled. "A patrolman volunteered to drive me back to Jefferson City. ... It was a trip I'll never forget. He drove more than 100 miles-per-hour along what was then an extremely narrow and curvy road. It seemed like we only hit the tops of hills as we flew along." [cccxliv]

As a result of the "Great Riot of 1954," the Department of Corrections was reorganized, guards changed from older, untrained men in street clothes to men in their prime wearing blue uniforms. New menus prepared in sanitary conditions were served in a modern dining room. High school diplomas were being earned and a full-time doctor was added to the hospital staff.

East had arrived in Jefferson City as a UPI legislative reporter in 1948, after a year's assignment in Dallas, Texas. [cccxlv]

In 1950, she became the first female bureau chief for a wire service in the U.S. [cccxlvi] The next five years included some of the most memorable events in the city's history, including the riot and the Hall-Heady execution. [cccxlvii]

Hall and his girlfriend Heady were convicted of kidnapping and murdering Bobby Greenlease, the son of a Kansas City Cadillac dealer. They were executed side-by-side in the only gas chamber double execution in Missouri history. [cccxlviii]

"Giffen was stationed outside the prison at a phone line that was a direct connection to United Press headquarters in New York. It was her job to keep the line open for United Press reporter Ward Caldwell to dictate a story after witnessing the execution as a pool reporter," Active Times said. [cccxlix]

UPI scored a big scoop on the AP, when they noticed Hall had a lipstick smear on his cheek. [cccl]

"Never before in the memory of local citizens has a case attracted such world-wide attention. Never has a woman paid the supreme penalty in the lethal gas chamber here," the Jefferson City Post Tribune reported Dec. 18, 1953. ccccli More intriguing was that Heady "clung to life for 2 minutes and 10 seconds longer than her companion," once the pellets emitting cyanide gas were dropped into a container of acid. ccclii

East was born in 1924 to Mervin, a World War I veteran, and Jerena (Wadlow) East at their Newcastle, Wyoming, homestead. cccliii The East family moved to Rolla, where her father opened a farm equipment business and gas station, when the Depression hit. cccliv

The constant in East's early years was a local library. By age 6, she had written her first novel and in high school at Rolla, she was assistant editor of the school newspaper. ccclv

To pay her way as a student at Drury College, Springfield, during World War II, she got a full-time scholarship as the first female editor of the student newspaper, The Drury Mirror.

Plus, East also took a job at a local radio station, writing the news read by broadcasters at KWTO and KGBX. ccclvi She found herself behind the microphone, however, to announce the death of President Franklin Roosevelt April 12, 1945. ccclvii

East worked part-time for the United Press office in Springfield and continued to work for UPI, when she transferred to the University of Missouri-Columbia School of Journalism for her senior year in 1946.

As a Mizzou J-school student, she was an assistant correspondent when Sir Winston Churchill gave his famed "Iron Curtain" speech at Westminster College, Fulton, and covered two sensational murder trials in Columbia – a man accused of killing a babysitter and a German professor who fed his French wife arsenic.

After graduation, she took a public relations job with Emerson Electric in St. Louis, but found it unrewarding and quickly returned to newspapers, despite the lower pay. ccclviii

After seven years with UPI in Jefferson City, East resigned following her marriage to local doctor Lawrence "Larry" Giffen, who was just beginning his practice.

Larry Giffen was born in 1923 in Jefferson City, graduated from St. Peters High School and then Jefferson City Junior College. In 1945, he graduated from Kirksville College of Osteopathy. He was a veteran of the Navy Medical Corps and was the first anesthesiologist at the newly-opened Charles E. Still Hospital.

After he retired in 1988, he spent four summers with the Indian Health Service in Montana. He also was elected two terms as the Cole County Coroner and then was appointed several years as Cole County Medical Examiner. ccclix

Later in life, he earned a bachelor's degree in history from the University of Maryland, a bachelor's degree in biology and a master's in history from Lincoln University, and a master's degree in criminal justice from Central Missouri State University, Warrensburg. [ccclx]

"Giffen chose to sacrifice her time-intensive career for the stability of her family," the News Tribune said. She said "leaving notes on the ice box did not work well. Our hectic schedules were not conducive to a young marriage." [ccclxi]

Wire service work never was free of deadlines and she often worked 12 hours a day. "I never regretted quitting. I couldn't have done both the job and raised a family," East-Giffen said. [ccclxii]

She reared their children Michael, born in 1958, and Jerena Ann, born in 1961. Michael died in a car accident at age 18. Daughter "Jan" graduated from the Grinnel College in Iowa and the London School of Economics. [ccclxiii] East-Giffen was involved in the parent-teacher organizations and served as a school room mother, as well as publishing an elementary school newspaper. In the late 1960s, she was director of information for the Greater Jefferson City Committee, reviewing and seeking solutions to major city problems and needs, such as parking, highways and public transportation. [ccclxiv]

In May 1969, she was secretary of the first Jefferson City Charter Commission. She was also on the Thomas Jefferson Regional Library board 1963-72, serving a term as president. Then, 1972-78 she served on the Jefferson City Board of Education, including terms as Treasurer and President. From 1984-86, she served on the United Way of Jefferson City Executive Committee. She also volunteered with the Community Concert Association, the Missouri Symphony Society, Girl Scouts and the Jefferson City Swim Club. [ccclxv]

East-Giffen returned to the workforce, doing publicity for the state health and social service departments. Then, she returned to school, earning a master's degree in public administration in 1980.

When her husband decided to fulfill his lifelong dream of joining the U.S. Navy, she decided to pursue her own dream of a Ph.D. While pursuing her 1989 doctorate in political science, she was a teaching assistant at MU, a graduate instructor at Lincoln University, an adjunct instructor at Columbia College and a visiting instructor at the University of Missouri-Rolla. [ccclxvi]

Then, she became an adjunct assistant professor at Lincoln University and at the University of Missouri-Rolla, plus teaching for Lincoln's adult program, Learning In Retirement. Courses she taught included political science, public policy, business administration and public administration. [ccclxvii]

In 2000, East-Giffen donated 2 cubic feet of her notes and papers, many prepared for her lessons, to the Missouri State Historic Society, Columbia, including her reporter's notebooks covering the Hall-Heady execution and the MSP riot. [ccclxviii]

Journalist, wife, mother, civic volunteer, professor – East-Giffen also added author to her many accomplishments.

Several pieces of Missouri's history have been preserved by her, including the Capital City's early education system and the state's first ladies.

"Writing is an artform; the skills are there, but must be developed. You must know what stirs the interest of your readers, what to emphasize," East-Giffen said. [ccclxix]

During the Jefferson City Public Schools' 1960s campaigns to build a new high school, the local school history was lean. School officials asked East-Giffen to do the research. [ccclxx]

Until that point, her writing had been paragraphs, not pages. [ccclxxi] "Had she known what she was getting into, (she) might not have agreed to research the sparse history of Jefferson City schools," a News Tribune article said. "Without Giffen's diligence of research and her solid journalism background … few in Jefferson City may have known the true tales behind Hobo Hill or Jay Hill." [ccclxxii]

She spent months at the state historical society reading hundreds of pages of local newspapers over a 150-year span. The schools had no written records until the 1900s.

The 288-page "House on Hobo Hill," her first book, was published in 1964 when the new high school opened. Local artist Robert Fredericks designed the original book jacket and chapter headings. "Plus Two for Jay Hill" was her third book, finished in 1975.

East-Giffen's second book was "First Ladies of Missouri: Their Homes and Their Families," completed in 1970 and

Photo courtesy Jefferson City News Tribune, Julie Smith

revised in 1996. She "thought first, the book should describe the influence of Missouri First Ladies on the state's history. But, somewhere along the line, 'I got so interested in their personalities. It's so hard to measure their influence,'" she said. [ccclxxiii]

In 1971, she contributed "Add a Pinch and a Lump: Missouri Women in the 1820s" to the Missouri Historical Review. And, that year she was named Author of the Year by the Missouri Writers Guild. ccclxxiv

She wrote "Charles E. Lee: A Biography" in 1999, the same year the Cole County Historical Society gave her the Hope Award.

After her husband's death in 1999, she finished the book, "Walks on Water: The Impact of Steamboats on the Lower Missouri River," based on Larry's work toward his sixth degree, proof of an insatiable love of learning. Giffen published what was to be Larry's dissertation for a PhD in history from MU. Larry's love for the Missouri River was encouraged by a river commute to his practice in Chamois and later living on a bluff overlooking the waterway on Hayselton Drive.

"Jere knew better than anyone how much this book meant to Larry. ... Jere resolved to complete the task," the Missouri State Archive finding aid said. ccclxxv

In 2002, she wrote "And Then There Were Twelve ... the history of the first Presbyterian Church of Jefferson City, Missouri."

Throughout her 54 years in Jefferson City, she was a devoted member of First Presbyterian Church, where she was an elder and deacon. There, she established a prayer shawl ministry, modeled after one she had been part of at the Congregational Church, Topsfield, Massachusetts. ccclxxvi

To write "Mary, Mary Quite ... The Life and Times of Mary Whitney Phelps 1812-1878," East-Giffen received the State Historical Society of Missouri's Brownlee Fund Grant in 2002.ccclxxvii

Born in Maine, Mary Whitney was the daughter of a sea captain and married John Phelps, a Connecticut attorney, in 1837. They later settled in Green County, where she stayed during her husband's gubernatorial term. Mary and her daughter rode the first Butterfield Stage trip across Mid-Missouri. ccclxxviii

In 2007, she was co-author for local banker Sam B. Cook Jr.'s autobiography. ccclxxix

Her 10th and final book was a children's book, "Smile, There's a Rainbow" in 2009. ccclxxx

East-Giffen moved closer to her daughter in 2002, leaving Jefferson City for Danvers, Massachusetts. She continued to write, even after moving into the Brooksby Village retirement community in Peabody, Massachusetts, until her death in 2016. ccclxxxi

10 SARAH MILDRED "MILLIE" PARSONS LINN STANDISH

Resilient Lady of Kindness and Service

- ❖ Born: Sept. 14, 1834, Charlottesville, Virginia
- ❖ Died: May 23, 1919, St. Louis, Missouri
- ❖ Notable: Matron of Missouri School for the Blind, won lawsuit with Mexican government for compensation for husband's murder

Mildred Standish saw more personal tragedy in her life than most people. Yet, she retained her southern dignity and grace, turning outward instead of inward.

All three of her sons preceded her in death, as did two husbands – the second murdered by the Mexican army soon after his release from parole at the end of the Civil War. And, she was the last of her siblings to pass away.

She built an historic city Landmark on Jackson Street, next to the one built by her father, Gen. Gustavus A. Parsons. And, she devoted decades of service the Missouri School for the Blind as matron and administrator.

She was born in 1834 in Charlottesville, Virginia, to Gen. Gustavus A. Parsons and Patience Monroe (Bishop) Parsons. [ccclxxxii] Siblings Mosby Monroe, Mary Ann, Eliza Jane, Frances Jackson and Virginia Terrill welcomed her. [ccclxxxiii]

Gustavus and Patience were married in 1821 in Charlottesville, Virginia. Gustavus was born in Henrico County, Virginia, in 1801 and orphaned by age 15. [ccclxxxiv] He studied law at Monticello, Virginia, at some point "employed by President Thomas Jefferson in some capacity in his office." [ccclxxxv]

The local legend says that the aged former president instructed young Parsons to go west to the city by his name. There may be some truth to this, as two men who claimed to be the president's nephews lived with the Parsons family in Jefferson City, one even marrying a daughter.

This sister, Mary Ann, died in 1844 at the home of Josiah Hodge in Osage County, at age 20, only months after marrying Merriwether Lewis Jefferson. Her obituary said "society has lost one of its brightest ornaments. Possessing firmness of mind, she bore her sickness with patience." ccclxxxvi

Gustavus Parsons had earned his military experience in Indian uprisings in the east, helping him serve twice as Missouri's adjutant general, 1843-48 and 1857-60. He was noted for personally riding to the Kansas Border in an attempt to settle the uprisings. ccclxxxvii

When Mildred was age 5, her family moved to Missouri, first in Cooper County and then, in 1837, to Jefferson City. ccclxxxviii As a brickmason, Gustavus first visited Jefferson City due to a contract, which fell through, to build a brick home for Judge George W. Miller. In 1839, her father was appointed deputy to E.L. Edwards, clerk of the circuit and county courts. Two years later, Gustavus was elected the successor, continuing in that position for 24 years.

"His first home here was a stone house, near the river and shortly afterwards he built a beautiful home on an eminence overlooking the Missouri. The spacious grounds extended from the house, across the present State Street long-known as Water Street, almost to Capitol Avenue. When Jackson and Water streets were cut through, the grounds were reduced in size and the long flight of stone steps removed." ccclxxxix

When Mildred was 12, her oldest brother, Mosby, left his law practice to volunteer for the Mexican-American War as a captain, commanding Company F of Col. Alexander Doniphan's Missouri Mounted Volunteers. cccxc

By 1850, Mildred was 16 and had lost two more older sisters. Living at her parents' home were Mosby and older sister Virginia; younger siblings Julia, Missouri and Gustavus Jr; her widowed brother-in-law Jefferson, who was county sheriff; plus three boarders – a clergyman, lawyer and merchant. cccxci

That same year, her brother, Mosby, married Mary Wells, daughter of local Judge Robert Wells, who designed the state seal, in 1850. They had son Stephen Kearney in 1851. However, Mary and baby Josephine both died shortly after the birth in 1853. cccxcii

At age 17, Mildred married her first husband, Dr. Henry "Duncan" Linn. He had been among a troupe of young beaus, including Ephraim Ewing, Green Clay Berry and Christy Watson. cccxciii They often went horseback riding with friends to fish and picnic. cccxciv

Linn was 26, and had studied at the University of Virginia. He returned to Missouri as a physician and also taught school. The couple had moved to Maries County for his practice, where he died only a few years later. cccxcv

In the meantime, sister Virginia married Green Clay Berry, also a Virginia native, in 1855. The couple built a nice brick home, still standing today, near the Moreau River on 350 acres.

Green C. Berry had been appointed deputy to Gustavus in the clerk's office and then served many years as collector and sheriff before his untimely death, the result of a Bagnell Branch train derailment near Russellville.

Mildred married March 10, 1857, Augustine "Austin" Martin Standish, an Irish immigrant, born June 14, 1826, at Cahara House County, Limerick, Ireland. He was an accomplished civil engineer, a gentleman of education and cultivation of fine personal appearance. [cccxcvi]

Austin Standish arrived in the U.S. in 1851 and his brother, Thomas, followed in 1854. [cccxcvii] The Standish brothers were sons of English Navy man, Richard Standish, and his wife, Elizabeth. The brothers both were civil engineers and Thomas would follow his older brother into the Confederacy. Austin was chief engineer for the Missouri Pacific Railroad for several years and was naturalized in 1859. [cccxcviii]

Mildred and Austin Standish had sons Richard and Austin D'Arcy in 1857 and 1859, respectively. In 1860, others living with them included the Jeffersons – Meriwether, whose property value was more than $25,000, and Robert, who worked at the Missouri State Penitentiary; as well as two boarders. [cccxcix]

When the Civil War broke out, Austin Standish followed Mildred's brother, Mosby Monroe Parsons, into the rebel Missouri Home Guards, later part of the Confederate States of America Army. M.M. Parsons must have been a man of charisma. As a states rights Democrat, he had served as U.S. district attorney, state representatives and state senator before the war began. [cd]

Having served in the war with Mexico, Gov. Claiborne Jackson commissioned M.M. Parsons as a brigadier general in the State Guards in 1861.

Mildred's husband, brother, and brother-in-law, Thomas, left Jefferson City with many other men from local, prominent, southern-sympathizing families. They arrived too late for the Battle of Boonville, after Gen. Sterling Price and Gov. Jackson fled the Capitol, due to arriving Union occupation. Gen. Parsons and Austin Standish fought at the Battle of Wilson's Creek, then went south to Arkansas with the Missouri rebel army.

From Camp Springfield in August 1861, M.M. Parsons wrote to his teen-aged son Kearney of the "trying scenes, scorching suns, bloods and bloody battle fields" he already had passed through. He lamented that Union soldiers in Jefferson City had ransacked their home and crushed mementos of their lost mother/wife, including her flower garden where campfires were then lit. [cdi]

Mildred's youngest brother, Gustavus Jr., died of disease, exhaustion and exposure on the eve of his 18th birthday. He was a Confederate lieutenant in Purdall's Sharpshooters and they had just marched from Prairie Grove, Arkansas, to Pea Ridge. The young Parsons had enlisted in the Missouri State Guard soon after his brother and brother-in-law left. [cdii]

"By his efficiency and judgement greatly contributed to the proficiency to which that brigade attained in the campaigning in Mississippi and Arkansas during the last summer," said the letter informing the family of his death. "His military attainments and officer-like conduct won the admiration of all his brother-officers and his unassuming manners and gentlemanly demeanor gained the esteem of his acquaintances." [cdiii]

Gov. Claiborne Jackson had given Austin Standish the rank of Colonel in the Missouri State Guard in June 1861. When he was transferred to the Confederate States of America's army, he was commissioned a Captain and appointed Chief of Staff for his brother-in-law in September 1862. He was appointed adjutant general in May 1863, while they were near Little Rock, Arkansas.

The division moved to Camp Bragg, Arkansas, by November 1863. Standish was assigned as division inspector general in March 1864 and the next month, Parson's Division fought at the Battle of Pleasant Hill, Louisiana, in April 1864. They were camped at Camden, Arkansas, in the fall of 1864.

At the end of the war, Standish and Parsons were paroled at Shreveport, Louisiana, as Prisoners of War after Gen. Kirby Smith surrendered to Union Maj. Gen. Canby.

Austin "fought bravely from the beginning to the end, escaping death when his horse was shot out under him, the fall crushing his watch, glasses and passed at the Battle of Wilsons Creek," his son recalled. [cdiv] At the Battle of Wilsons Creek, his pocket watch stopped a mini ball. He was taken prisoner, but was able to slip away in the chaos. [cdv] At the Battle of Pleasant Hill, Louisiana, he again was wounded, this time in the hand. [cdvi]

When President Abraham Lincoln was elected to a second term in November 1864, Mildred's father "advised me to go south and try to persuade my husband Col. Standish to leave the Confederate Army and take a position of less danger than that of chief of staff to my brother, Gen. Monroe M. Parsons. It was no lack of devotion to the Confederate cause, so dear to the heart of every southern woman, that impelled me to make the effort to save further risk of life to my husband and the father of my three small sons." [cdvii]

Richard Adolphus was 3 and Austin D'Arcy an infant when their father went to war. Mildred may not have known yet that she was pregnant with Monroe Parsons in the spring of 1861.

"I started on my mission early in December 1864 from Jefferson City arriving in St. Louis to join a party of ladies from Lexington … and Boonville on their way to the Southern Confederacy." Traveling with her three boys, ages 2 to 7, she expected to travel by boat, but an ice-covered Mississippi River changed her plans to rail. [cdviii]

She found southern-sympathizers along the way to help her along. While loading the train, a man repaired one her trunks, he said "I know who you are and will care for your baggage. I am a Confederate soldier from Gen. Parson's camp at Camden, Arkansas." [cdix]

Once they were seated in the railroad car, an attractive man sat nearby. After judging she could confide her secret travel plans with him, "he told me he had a fine boat leaving Cairo the next day and would like us to go with him." Mrs. Standish cautioned he might not want their party; "we are all rebels on our way to the Southern Confederacy," she told him. His whispered reply was: "That is just the kind I like." [cdx]

The four Standish family members, as well as the other ladies, decided to board Captain Cabels' boat, the Niagara. "We could not have had a safer and more interesting trip all of the officers looking after our comfort and pleasure and enjoying dancing and playing cards with the ladies." [cdxi]

She found kindness for her efforts, even from a Union captain. When their trunks were searched, the officer asked: "What have you got in your trunks for your husband?" When she said, "nothing," the officer replied: "I know better. If I were down there in the Southern army, my wife would risk being arrested to bring something to me." Then, the jolly man closed her trunks without searching to the bottom. [cdxii]

On the way, the Niagara stopped at Helena, Arkansas, where her brother's soldiers had been victorious in the great battle there. She was met by Union Gen. Francis J. Herron, who had been in charge of the federal gunboats opposite her brother. "He received me most cordially, saying ... 'I met your brave brother in battle, later conferring with him about the wounded prisoners. I never knew a braver or better man.'" [cdxiii]

Mrs. Standish and her boys departed the Niagara at the mouth of the White River. She bid farewell to the friends they had made and her passage money was returned to her by the ship's clerk. She refused a further offer of money, thinking she could cover her expenses with Confederate money. [cdxiv]

However, neither was Confederate money accepted, nor her passes honored. In Missouri, she was given a pass that should have taken her to Confederate Gen. Daniel Reynolds in Little Rock. But, Union Gen. George McGinnis at the White River did not let them go until he heard directly from Gen. Reynolds. While there, a Col. Campbell from Ohio "took such a fancy to me because I looked like his dead wife, dead 6 months." The young Standish family waited two weeks aboard government boats, before a cart and baggage wagon were supplied for their trek to Little Rock. [cdxv]

On the journey, she learned that federal soldiers had burned their driver's home. At the beginning, he said "I fear you ladies will have trouble going through the swamp. It is infested by outlaws from both the federal and confederate armies." Instead, their wheel became stuck on the road and they were rescued by southern gentlemen on horseback. [cdxvi]

They were taken to the Bonnie Plantation to spend the night. Mrs. Standish's escort, Captain Crute of the Confederate cavalry, asked about General Price's raid when he learned she was from Jefferson City. In particular, he was interested in his best friend, Major Bonnie, son of their host. [cdxvii]

The wounded from the Mid-Missouri engagements of September 1864, were taken to Gustavus and Patience Parsons' home, but he was not among them. Mrs. Standish shared that Major Bonnie was killed in a skirmish at the Moreau River, just outside the Capital City. The sad news had not reached the Bonnie family. Perhaps they were comforted knowing the major had been buried on the farm of Mrs. Standish's brother-in-law, Green C. Berry. [cdxviii]

Capt. Crute continued to escort Mrs. Standish and her party through the woods to Monticello, a nearly-deserted town where they waited several days for transportation to Gen. Parson's camp at Camden, Arkansas. Here, Mrs. Standish saw her husband for the first time in more than 3 years and he, for the first time, saw his youngest son. Their travel was slow, rough and their stops sometimes unwelcome. [cdxix]

"My brother was not pleased, when he learned my object in coming, but my husband, seeing our helplessness, was willing to take a place on General (John) Magruder's staff of the artillery, where the danger would not be so great." [cdxx]

In celebration, Mrs. Standish managed to prepare a dinner, relying on military camp rations. She got a country ham from the commissary and Gen. Parsons contributed three ducks. She also had cake and coffee, which she brought from home. "No doubt it was very enjoyable in comparison to the meager fare of the officers mess table." Afterward, they observed the soldiers on dress parade. [cdxxi]

While in camp, Mrs. Standish was asked by her brother to patch a pair of his pantaloons, which had lost his seat. About the same time, Parsons wrote home to his son, Stephen Kearney, that "Milly, Rich, Stan and Monroe … are all in good health and are content in Dixie." [cdxxii]

Late winter 1865, Gen. Parsons moved his division to Collinsburg, Louisiana. Mrs. Standish was invited to stay at the plantation of Dr. Sandage, who had cared for her husband after he was wounded at the Battle of Pleasant Hill. [cdxxiii]

Mrs. Standish arrived in the division's new camp one night, in time to hear the late-night currier's horn bringing news of Gen. Robert E. Lee's April 9, 1865, surrender to Gen. Ulysses Grant at Appamattox Courthouse, Virginia. "Gloom spread throughout the camp and men were at a loss what to do." [cdxxiv]

Her brother, however, "decided at once to leave the country, believing that better opportunities of practicing their professions could be found elsewhere." After staying out all that night, her husband returned in the morning, to tell her of their plan to leave the country. She was given a choice to go with them, but she turned it down. [cdxxv]

Mrs. Standish continued to try to dissuade her husband, who replied: "Did you ever know me to decide to do a thing and then not do it? Do you suppose we are afraid of a few Mexicans after what we've been through?" [cdxxvi]

Many soldiers agreed to join their party at the beginning. But, it soon dwindled down to Parsons and Standish, Col. Aaron Hackett Conrow of Ray County, and William Wenderling, known as "Dutch Bill."[cdxxvii] The latter was from Callaway County and served as Standish's orderly, taking care of provisions for the group. [cdxxviii]

Conrow was born in Cincinnati, Ohio, and moved to Missouri at the age of 16. He studied law with a Supreme Court judge and was elected to the General Assembly in 1860. In Ray County, he was master of the Richmond Lodge, he was a circuit attorney, judge of the court of common pleas, public administrator and county treasurer. Then, during the war, his fellow soldiers elected him to the Confederate Congress and then he returned to the army. [cdxxix]

After the war's end announcement, the Parson's division moved to Shreveport, Louisiana, and Mrs. Standish and family with them. "Here we learned of the assassination of President Lincoln, much regret was expressed, everyone believing this death a calamity for the south." [cdxxx]

In his last letter home to his mother and father, Gen. Parsons wrote that he was a POW "not by consent or choice … There are other countries where I can yet claim to be a man to someone of them. I will go, and under the wing of its protection, recuperate my fallen fortunes. [cdxxxi]

"My destination is Mexico first, and then Brazil. I have not the means to take me anywhere, but must procure them first from funds at what was once my home or accept of the given city of strangers for settlement by Missourians. I will make myself a citizen of the empire, come home with my free papers in my pocket and let my friends know what are my views and opinions, as to what can be done for immigrants to that country." [cdxxxii]

With her husband committed to following her brother's quest to find better opportunities south of the border, Mrs. Standish left for home on a Tuesday and the men went in the other direction. After a perilous trip down the Red River, she and her sons arrived in New Orleans, hoping to return with her friend Captain Cabel aboard the Niagara. But, it had departed the day before. [cdxxxiii]

Despite having little money for the journey home, Mrs. Standish retained her dignity as a southern lady and would not take $50 offered to her by her escort, Colonel Ganse, to cover hotel and boat passage. The next day, the hotel surprised her, saying they had no bill against her. [cdxxxiv]

The day continued its surprises, when she discovered that John

Hamilton, who had been clerk on the Niagara, was now clerk of the only boat headed to St. Louis from New Orleans that day, the U.S. Arthur. "I had a delightful trip and when, I reached St. Louis, had as much money in my purse as when I left New Orleans." [cdxxxv]

At Union Station in St. Louis, she was given a pass to Jefferson City, courtesy of George R. Taylor, a Missouri Pacific official who had been a friend and coworker of her husband. The Missouri Pacific Railroad was going to charge Mrs. Standish $300, because Col. Standish had been in command of men who burned the railroad's bridges. Still, she was delayed another week before receiving a pass. [cdxxxvi]

"In view of the fact that I had not asked any favors, good fortune meeting me at every point was most remarkable. Surely a kind of providence guided me to find friends among strangers to help me through the difficult places." [cdxxxvii]

"She spent much of the time during the unpleasantness with her husband and brother and experienced many of the hardships of war unknown to most women," her obituary said. [cdxxxviii]

After returning home to Jefferson City in the summer of 1865, Mrs. Standish soon received news that her husband and brother had been murdered early in their quest.

Just before leaving Shreveport, Louisiana, Gen. Parsons wrote the sentiments of his part: "Though beaten, I am not subdued. I intend ever to feel, act and speak as a free man. ... There are other countries where I can yet claim to be a man. To some one of them I will go, and under the wing of its protection, recuperate my fallen fortunes."

The general had gained passports and permission from the Union authorities for his party to depart Aug. 12, 1865, for Brazil. [cdxxxix] Three days later, they had camped just crossed the San Juan River, after passing through Chino, Mexico. [cdxl]

Here, Parsons, Standish, Conrow and Dutch Bill were murdered by Mexican soldiers and their possessions stolen. It is likely their bodies were discovered by the townspeople, who built "four rude crosses." [cdxli] The John Wayne movie, *The Undefeated*, was loosely based on this doomed mission.

R.H. Musser gathered sworn statements from witnesses on behalf of the widows and heirs of these men and presented their case to the commission organized under the joint treaty of July 4, 1868.[cdxlii]

That included the account of Gen. John B. Clark Sr., who was traveling with another party, who camped nearby the Parsons-Standish party the evening of Aug. 15, 1865. They heard the shots fired and the next morning, Clark's company rode into the Parsons-Standish camp to find 20 dead Mexicans and no American bodies. [cdxliii]

Clarke said he found "significant marks of resistance of brave men whom only numbers could overpower." [cdxliv] Then, they "discovered the trails on the ground along which bodies had been dragged to the bank of the San Juan and cast into the river. Gen. Parsons had horses and equipages, a gold watch, and he was also known to have $4,000 in gold, which was gobbled up by the Mexicans," the Kansas City Times reported. [cdxlv]

Civil engineer Martin Van Merrick had traveled part way with the Parsons-Standish party. While in Chino, soon after the attack, Van Merrick saw some of the murderers, who had Parsons' horse, coat, pistol and other items and overheard them "boasting how they had killed him and his companions. [cdxlvi]

Col. Planton Sanchez, private secretary to Mexican Gen. Canales, and Capt. Dario Garza were among the Mexican soldiers presumed to have committed the crime. Later, Sanchez had Parsons' watch. Jesus Tyerina had some of the victims' clothing and Standish's engineering instruments. And, Lt. Nicholas Alanis had Parsons' pistol. [cdxlvii]

A Mr. Sillers worked at the American consulate at Vera Cruz and mounted an investigation that rebutted attempted alibis by the Mexican officers. Sillers had interviewed Planton Sanchez in 1866. "While in his cups," the Mexican officer "admitted he commanded the party who killed the Americans and exhibited as a trophy of the exploit the watch which belonged to Gen. Parsons," the Kansas City Times said. [cdxlviii]

"The Mexicans supposed or claimed to believe that Parsons party were enemies and the spies of Archduke Maximilian but on finding their mistake the commander ordered his troops to keep silence with regard to the death of these foreigners, because they had been killed under a belief that they were spies and they wanted it to be thought they were so," the Kansas City Times said. [cdxlix]

"I think if a government will keep such officers and soldiers in its pay and employment and make no effort to discover or punish their monstrous crime, even when they wear the effects of their victims before the eyes of their superiors, why that it should be held responsible for their conduct," W.H. Wadsworth said in the later lawsuit of the survivors versus the Mexican government. [cdl]

The lawsuit was under the U.S. Secretary of State John Ingle was umpired by Sir Edward Thornton, the British Minister in Washington D.C., in 1874.

The Mexican commissioner, Manuel Maria de Yamacona, said the circumstances could not be determined beyond crimes of common order for which the government would not be responsible. "There is nothing in it showing that in this case there was, on the part of the Mexican government, the knowledge of the facts and deliberate and indolent neglect which might produce a responsibility for private crimes on the part of the public authority." [cdli]

The umpire, Sir Thornton, reviewed the evidence and was convinced Col. Sanchez had given the order for the attack on the travelers. He noted the party's identity could have been confused, but it was still the failure of the Mexican officers to "discover the real character of the party attacked." [cdlii] Whether evil intentioned or not, the umpire declared the victims' families out to be compensated by the Mexican government for their loss. [cdliii]

Mildred Standish was awarded $40,000 Mexican gold dollars plus $1,500 annually with interest, calculated by the $2,500 annual income Col. Standish could have made as a civil engineer, plus compensation for the property taken at the time of the murder. [cdliv]

Also widowed with four young children, Mary Ann Conrow was awarded $50,000 and $300 annually with interest, because the "gains of Conrow as a lawyer were greater," Thornton said. [cdlv]

And for Stephen "Kearney" Parsons, Mildred's nephew, who was age 14 at his father's murder, Thornton awarded $50,000 and $500 annually with interest. Kearney studied at William Jewell College. He was a deputy sheriff in Jefferson City and later a guard at the Missouri State Penitentiary. He died of bronchitis and pneumonia in January 1889. He was known "to be a liberal and social gentleman," the Cole County Democrat said. [cdlvi]

The Standish, Parsons and Conrow families could not move on from the legal issues, despite the rulings in their favor in 1874. The lawyers who represented them before the Mexican claims commission, then wanted their share of the gold compensation. The suit by the lawyers versus the survivors of the murder victims went all the way to the U.S. Supreme Court in 1885.

"Several awards were made by the Mexican Claims Commission under the treaty between the United States and Mexico of July 4, 1868, in favor of claimants, representatives respectively of three American citizens – Parsons, Conrow and Standish, which amounted in the aggregate to $143,812.32. … Of this, half was paid to the claimants and the other half remained, with their consent, under the control of the Secretary of State to be paid to the agents and counsel of the claimants, according to their respective rights and interests," Justice Stanley Matthews said in his opinion.

While dealing with the legal matters, which stretched across three decades, Mildred Standish still had sons to raise and worked to provide for them.

In 1870, she was keeping the Wagner Hotel, which stood on the north side of the 100 block of West High Street, and her personal property was valued at $2,200. The 12 boarders at the time of the U.S. Census included a doctor and his family, local merchants, railroad workers, printers and painters. And four employees also lived there. [cdlvii]

After 1877, she divided her time between the home she grew up in and her decades of service at the Missouri School for the Blind in St. Louis. The institution, not an asylum, furnished "a clean and comfortable abode for destitute blind girls, who are out of employment, where useful occupations suitable to their capacities can be supplied them until they can secure situations in the meantime be nearly or quite self-sustaining," the St. Louis Globe Democrat said. [cdlviii]

The school at 20th and Morgan streets, St. Louis, held a fair and festival to raise money in December 1877. "Mrs. Mildred Standish, matron of the institution, was to be seen everywhere aiding and assisting all who needed her services. She found time, however, to show the reporter over the building, including the sleeping rooms, library, laundry, kitchen and dining room, the latter being under the especial care of Miss Theresa Hambourg, whom the matron declared was the neatest and cleanest person she ever saw," the St. Louis Globe Democrat reported. [cdlix]

"(Her) rare executive ability is due to neatness and order observed on every hand. ... Her gentleness and uniform kindness won the love and respect of all the inmates of the institute and her presence in the building is a guarantee that all is well," school committee chairman J.P.H. Gray told the General Assembly in 1881. [cdlx]

Her father, Gustavus, died at age 80 in 1882. A long-time county clerk, he trained his grandson, Richard to take over the office.

Standish Home on Jackson Street. Photo courtesy the Missouri State Archives Summers Collection.

Gustavus Parsons "was a pioneer and little of public interest has occurred in the county in the past 47 years in which he was not a participant," his obituary said. The officers of Cole County drafted a commemorative resolution for him, saying "the state has lost a valuable and honorable citizen and the county a faithful and upright officer ... he was ever conspicuous for his unswerving honesty and fidelity." [cdlxi]

"Though always poor himself, his charities were numerous and unostentatious. He found much pleasure in aiding with his means and fatherly advice many poor and otherwise helpless young men during his long and eventful life. From under his wise tutelage and out of his office, Congressman, Attorneys General, state senators, clerks and lawyers emerged, armed for successful conflict in life's great battle. Many a poor widow and many a wandering troop have been the recipients of his substantial benefactions," the People's Tribune said. [cdlxii]

Mildred's son, Richard, followed his grandfather as clerk of Cole County in January 1873. He was then elected to the post in November 1873, over Judge Phillip Ott. "He was very popular and held in high esteem. ... He was a young man of great promise and sterling worth." [cdlxiii] He died in October 1884 of consumption.

Just a few months before, Mildred's mother, Patience, had died, preceded in death by five of her nine children. "She was honored and reverenced by the entire community," Patience's obituary said. "She was at all times quiet, unassuming and generous to a fault." [cdlxiv]

Mildred Standish lost her other two sons in 1890.

Her middle son, Austin, was a top student for Prof. Nitchy in Jefferson City and moved to St. Louis University in 1877 when his mother went to work at the School for the Blind. He was recognized for diligent study and excellent deportment. He went on to McDowell Medical College, St. Louis, graduating in March 1881. He worked in St. Louis at the City Hospital and the Female Hospital, before opening a practice in January 1883 in Lincoln, Nebraska, where his aunt and Mildred's sister, Julia Trickey, lived. [cdlxv]

Austin returned to Jefferson City in June 1884 to help care for his brother, Richard, in the last months of his illness. In February 1885, Gov. John S. Marmaduke appointed him to a four-year term as the physician at the Missouri State Prison. But he did not complete that term, moving to Colorado, where he died in November 1890. [cdlxvi]

Mildred's youngest son, Monroe, had died six months earlier in Springfield, Missouri. Showing an early aptitude in math, Monroe arrived as a student at St. Louis University, while his mother worked at the School for the Blind. After graduation, he worked as a clerk and salesman for Richardson Drug Company and later Hopkins-Weller Drug Company. [cdlxvii]

After a decade of loss, Standish did quite a bit of traveling in the 1890s, visiting her sister in Nebraska, her niece, Mrs. William D'Oench in St.

Louis; Philadelphia, Pennsylvania; Canada and the World's Fair in Chicago, Illinois. cdlxviii

In 1898, Mildred was chaperone for young maids headed to Atlanta, Georgia, for the Daughters of the Confederacy national reunion. Mrs. Standish was described as "a sweet-faced, low-voiced woman in a dress of dove-gray, with white vest." cdlxix

She escorted three maids from Jefferson City – Ethel Edwards, Kitty E. Pitts and Mary Gantt -- to St. Louis, where they joined another 13 ladies from Missouri at the Lindell Hotel. "Old-time southern hospitality was dispensed" for the "gathering of beauties" from Missouri, Oklahoma and Indian Territory before they boarded the train south. cdlxx

When her sister, Julia Trickey, died in 1908, Mildred was the last survivor of her notable family. cdlxxi

When St. Mary's Hospital was destroyed by fire Feb. 20, 1919, Mildred had been among the 75 patients evacuated safely. The fire swept up an elevator shaft and throughout the building. cdlxxii

Mildred was taken to the home of Mr. and Mrs. John Giesecke and then she went to stay with her niece, Nancy Berry D'Oench, in St. Louis. cdlxxiii There she died a few months later.

Her obituary called her a "most excellent woman" and she was one of the oldest members of Grace Episcopal Church. cdlxxiv

In her will, she left half of her estate to niece Nancy Berry D'Oench and the other half to be divided between nephews John, R.L. and Frank Berry and Adolphus and Paul Turner. She left jewelry to niece on her husband's side Elizabeth, Glynn and Mattie Standish, as well as other extended family Mildred and Robert Berry. Some money also was set aside for repairs to the family monument and cemetery lot at the Woodland-Old City Cemetery on McCarty Street and for reconstruction of streets abutting the cemetery. As for the home on Jackson Street, Church Realty sold it for $4,750. cdlxxv

"Although crushed by double tragedy which came to her as the result of the war, and it's subsequent financial responsibilities, Mrs. Standish faced the future with grace and dignity which caused her to be one of the most beloved personages of the city." cdlxxvi

Index

ABOUT THE AUTHORS

Michelle Brooks spent more than 20 years writing for Missouri newspapers, the last 19 with Central Missouri Newspapers Inc. In that time, she garnered more than 100 industry awards for her writing, predominantly in history and faith matters. After earning a Bachelor's Degree in Liberal Studies, with emphasis in anthropology and history, from Lincoln University in 2018, she joined the Missouri State Archive, where she is a research analyst. Her first book was "Hidden History of Jefferson City" published by The History Press in 2021.

As Chief Museum Interpreter for the Missouri State Museum – located inside the Capitol - and a lifelong Missouri resident, **Carrie Mackey Hammond** spends her workdays connecting museum visitors to the state's cultural and natural resources through education, outreach, and local partnerships. In Carrie's leisure time, she can be found at a Missouri State Parks campsite or at her rural home in Osage County which she shares with her beloved partner, her son with special needs, and numerous pets.

END NOTES

CHAPTER 1

[i] Ford, James Everett. *A History of Jefferson City, Missouri's State Capital, and of Cole County*. New Day Press. p 527. 1938.

[ii] Abel, A.A.E. *Abel's Photographic Weekly*. Vol. 27. Page 492. 1921.

[iii] *Jefferson City Post Tribune*. September 5, 1924.

[iv] Bee County (Texas) Historical Society Facebook page.

[v] *Beeville (Texas) Bee-Picayune*. Aug. 3, 1967.

[vi] Chambers, Frank V. *Bulletin of Photographer*, Vol. 21. P172. 1917.

[vii] *Daily Capital News (Jefferson City, Mo.)*. September 1, 1921.

[viii] *Daily Capital News (Jefferson City, Mo.)*. March 22, 1922.

[ix] *Jefferson City Post Tribune*. June 8, 1929.

[x] *Sunday News and Tribune (Jefferson City, Mo.)*. June 9, 1935.

[xi] Ford. *A History of Jefferson City*.

[xii] Johnston, J.W. *The Illustrated Sketch Book and Directory of Jefferson City and Cole County*. Missouri Illustrated Sketch Book Company. 1900.

[xiii] Cole County Historical Society Museum. Photographer Biographical Sketches.
www.colecountyhistoricalmuseum.org/photographers-biographical-sketches

[xiv] Beetem, Jane. "Broadway-Dunklin Historic District." National Register of Historic Places (Washington, D.C., U.S. Department of the Interior. National Park Service.). 2002.

[xv] "Photographer is an ideal business for women." Women in Business. *Kansas City Star*. Oct. 12, 1924.

[xvi] Ibid.

[xvii] *Jefferson City Post Tribune*. Feb. 23, 1932.

[xviii] *Daily Capital News (Jefferson City, Mo.)*. May 15, 1928.

[xix] Ibid.

[xx] *Jefferson City Post Tribune*. March 31, 1936.

[xxi] *Sunday News and Tribune (Jefferson City, Mo.)*. Aug. 30, 1936.

[xxii] *Jefferson City Post-Tribune*. Dec. 5, 1930.

[xxiii] Ibid.

[xxiv] Ford. *A History of Jefferson City*.

[xxv] *Daily Capital News (Jefferson City, Mo.)*. May 9, 1929.

[xxvi] *St. Louis Globe Democrat*. March 19, 1935.

[xxvii] *Beeville (Texas) Bee-Picayune*. Aug. 3, 1967.

[xxviii] Ibid.

[xxix] 1930 U.S. Federal Census. Jefferson City, Cole County, Missouri. Page 4A. Enumeration District 0008.

[xxx] *Jefferson City Post Tribune*. June 28, 1930.

[xxxi] Ibid.

[xxxii] 1940 U.S. Federal Census. Jefferson City, Cole County, Missouri. Page 3B. Enumeration District 26-9.

[xxxiii] Ruth Rust Death Certificate. Missouri Death Certificates, 1910-1970. Missouri State Archives, Jefferson City. 1937.

CHAPTER 2

xxxiv Aycock, Rebekah. "The Women's Suffrage Movement in Kansas City." The Pendergast Years. The Kansas City Public Library.

xxxv Ford. *A History of Jefferson City*. p543.

xxxvi Ibid.

xxxvii *History of Cole, Moniteau, Morgan, Benton, Miller, Maries and Osage counties, Missouri*. Goodspeed Publishing Company, Chicago. 1889.

xxxviii Ibid.

xxxix Ibid

xl Van Nada, M.L. *The Book of Missourians*. T.J. Steele, Chicago. 1906.

xli Dallmeyer, Alvin. Letter to the Editor. *The Sunday News and Tribune* (Jefferson City). Jan. 27, 1957.

xlii Van Nada. *The Book of Missourians*.

xliii Johnston. *The Illustrated sketch book*.

xliv "Mrs. Frank E. Shelden, President of the Twentieth Century Club." Pen-point Portraits of Kansas City Women. *The Kansas City Star*. Aug. 18, 1929.

xlv Ford. *A History of Jefferson City*. p543.

xlvi "Art Club." Undated clipping. Mathilde Dallmeyer Shelden scrapbook. Jackson County Historical Society.

xlvii "Music Club." Undated clipping. Mathilde Dallmeyer Shelden scrapbook. Jackson County Historical Society.

xlviii "Woman sells $10,000 war stamps in one day." *St. Louis Globe Democrat*. April 6, 1918

xlix "Mrs. Frank E. Shelden." *The Kansas City Star*. 1929.

l "Woman sells $10,000 war stamps in one day." *St. Louis Globe Democrat*. April 6, 1918.

li Dallmeyer, Alvin. Letter to the Editor. *The Sunday News and Tribune* (Jefferson City, Mo.). Jan. 27, 1957.

lii *Daily Capital News* (Jefferson City, Mo.). April 12, 1918.

liii "Mrs. Frank E. Shelden. *The Kansas City Star*. 1929.

liv Flynn, Jane Fifield. *Kansas City Women of Independent Minds*. Fifield Publishing Company. 1992.

lv Ibid.

lvi "State Suffragists Elect Mrs. Boyd." *St. Louis Globe-Democrat*. April 5, 1913.

lvii "She gets job to work out theory." *St. Joseph Gazette*. May 28, 1915.

lviii Ibid.

lix Blackwell, Alice Stone. *The Woman Citizen*. Leslie Woman Suffrage Commission. 1917.

lx "Mrs. Frank E. Shelden. *The Kansas City Star*. 1929.

lxi *The Kansas City Times*. July 9, 1920.

lxii Ford. *A History of Jefferson City*. p543.

lxiii "Congressman Dyer in clash with a negro." *Chillicothe Constitution Tribune*. July 28, 1919.

lxiv "Republican Steam roller: Flattens all opposition – Miss Dallmeyer is punished for lead on machine method." *The Daily Capital News* (Jefferson City, Mo.). May 7, 1920.

lxv Ibid.

lxvi Ibid.

lxvii Martyn, Marguerite. "Women's Belief in Suffrage Firmer Than Ever, Despite Differences at Convention." *St. Louis Post-Dispatch*. May 9, 1920.

[lxviii] *The Kansas City Times*. July 9, 1920.

[lxix] Flynn. 1992.

[lxx] "Killed when car skids." *The Kansas City Times*. July 5, 1924.

[lxxi] Ibid.

[lxxii] Ibid

[lxxiii] "Evangelicals pass resolution of sympathy." *The Daily Capital News* (Jefferson City, Mo.). July 15, 1924.

[lxxiv] "Death of Mrs. Frank Shelden." *The Kansas City Star*. Dec. 2, 1918.

[lxxv] "Dr. Frank E. Shelden." *The Kansas City Times*. Jan. 6, 1966.

[lxxvi] Ibid.

[lxxvii] "Mrs. Frank E. Shelden, *The Kansas City Star*. 1929.

[lxxviii] "Death of Mrs. Frank Shelden." *The Kansas City Star*. Dec. 2, 1918.

[lxxix] "Mrs. Frank E. Shelden. *The Kansas City Star*. 1929.

[lxxx] Flynn. 1992.

[lxxxi] Ibid.

[lxxxii] Ford. *A History of Jefferson City*. p543.

[lxxxiii] Green, George Fuller. *A Condensed History of the Kansas City Area: Its Mayors and Some V.I.P.s.* The Lowell Press. 1968.

CHAPTER 3

[lxxxiv] "The Lady's Legacy Lives." Unknown magazine. Lincoln University Archive.

[lxxxv] Ibid.

[lxxxvi] *Daily Capital News* (Jefferson City, Mo.). Oct. 22, 1942.

[lxxxvii] *Daily Capital News* (Jefferson City, Mo.). Oct. 23, 1942.

[lxxxviii] *Kansas City Times*. Oct. 24, 1942.

[lxxxix] *St. Louis Post-Dispatch*. Oct. 24, 1942.

[xc] "Negro band shuns parade." *Kansas City Times*. Oct. 24, 1942.

[xci] "The Lady's Legacy Lives." Unknown magazine. Lincoln University Archive.

[xcii] "Tribune paid service men." *Lincoln Clarion* (Jefferson City, Mo.). Nov. 13, 1942.

[xciii] Ibid.

[xciv] Ibid.

[xcv] Ibid.

[xcvi] Ibid.

[xcvii] Fletcher, Thomas T. *The Lincoln Clarion* (Jefferson City, Mo.). May 28, 1943.

[xcviii] "The Lady's Legacy Lives." Unknown magazine. Lincoln University Archive.

[xcix] *Lincoln Clarion* (Jefferson City, Mo.). April 27, 1945.

[c] *Lincoln Clarion* (Jefferson City, Mo.). Oct 26, 1945.

[ci] *Lincoln Clarion* (Jefferson City, Mo.). Feb. 20, 1948.

[cii] Ibid.

[ciii] Ibid.

[civ] Ibid.

[cv] Ibid.

[cvi] Ibid.

[cvii] *Lincoln Clarion* (Jefferson City, Mo.). May 7, 1948.

[cviii] *The Moberly Monitor-Index*. May 4, 1948.

[cix] *Lincoln Clarion* (Jefferson City, Mo.). May 7, 1948.

[cx] *The Moberly Monitor-Index*. May 4, 1948.

[cxi] Supreme.Justia.com U.S. Supreme Court case Sipuel v. Board of Regents. (1948)
[cxii] *St. Louis Post-Dispatch.* Feb. 25, 1951.
[cxiii] Ibid.
[cxiv] "The Lady's Legacy Lives." Unknown magazine. Lincoln University Archive.
[cxv] *St. Louis Post-Dispatch.* Feb. 25, 1951.
[cxvi] "The Lady's Legacy Lives." Unknown magazine. Lincoln University Archive.
[cxvii] Ibid.
[cxviii] *Lincoln Clarion* (Jefferson City, Mo.). March 28, 1952.
[cxix] "The Lady's Legacy Lives." Unknown magazine. Lincoln University Archive.
[cxx] Ibid.
[cxxi] Parks, Arnold. *History of Lincoln: 1920-1970.* Arcadia Publishing. 2007.
[cxxii] "The Lady's Legacy Lives." Unknown magazine. Lincoln University Archive.
[cxxiii] Ibid.
[cxxiv] Ibid.
[cxxv] Ibid.
[cxxvi] Ibid.
[cxxvii] *Lincoln Clarion* (Jefferson City). Nov. 20, 1953.
[cxxviii] Ibid.
[cxxix] Ibid.
[cxxx] "The Lady's Legacy Lives." Unknown magazine. Lincoln University Archive.
[cxxxi] Ibid.

CHAPTER 4

Carlisle (Pennsylvania) Weekly Herald. Page 1. Dec. 5, 1881.
Omaha (Nebraska) Daily Bee. Oct. 10, 1881.
The Black Hills Daily Times, Deadwood, South Dakota. Page 2. Oct. 22, 1881.
The Republican Farmer, Loudon, Tennessee. Page 3. Feb. 2, 1882.
The San Francisco (California) Examiner. Page 1. Sept. 18, 1881.
U.S. Census. Nevada.

CHAPTER 5

[cxxxii] *Marshall Daily Democrat News.* June 12, 1909.
[cxxxiii] Ibid.
[cxxxiv] "Grace Hershey." *Lawrence (Kansas) Daily World.* Aug. 11, 1910.
[cxxxv] Ibid.
[cxxxvi] "Joins Red Cross." *Abilene (Kansas) Weekly Reflector.* Sept. 5, 1918.
[cxxxvii] Ibid.
[cxxxviii] "Abilene girl wins typewriting contest." *Abilene (Kansas) Weekly Reflector.* Oct. 30, 1913.
[cxxxix] "Biographical Sketches of Early Cole County Residents." Cole County Historical Society and Museum. Retrieved March 6, 2021.
[cxl] "New home of the Thorpe J. Gordon Funeral Service." *Jefferson City Post-Tribune*. Aug. 18, 1938.
[cxli] U.S. Army Transport Service Passenger lists, 1910-1939. Ancestry.com.
[cxlii] "Joins Red Cross." *Abilene (Kansas) Weekly Reflector.* Sept. 5, 1918.
[cxliii] Holt, Marilyn. "Women as Casualties of World War I and Spanish Influenza: A Kansas Study." *Kansas History: A Journal of the Central Plains.* 2017.

cxliv "Gave her life." *Abilene (Kansas) Daily Reflector.* Nov. 10, 1922.
cxlv "Grace Hershey in France." *The Abilene (Kansas) Weekly Chronicle.* Oct. 23, 1918.
cxlvi "Help in Canteens." *The Salina (Kansas) Evening Journal.* Nov. 4, 1918.
cxlvii "The Comforting Words of Lincoln." *Abilene (Kansas) Weekly Chronicle.* Nov. 6, 1918.
cxlviii "World War I and the American Red Cross." American Red Cross. www.redcross.org
cxlix Amick, Jeremy P. *Jefferson City At War: 1916-1975.* Images of America. Arcadia Publishing. 2014.
cl "Memorial to Miss Hershey." *Abilene (Kansas) Weekly Chronicle.* April 26, 1922.
cli "The Honor Roll." *Abilene (Kansas) Daily Chronicle.* Aug. 22, 1922.
clii "Gave her life." *Abilene (Kansas) Daily Reflector.* Nov. 10, 1922.
cliii "161 American Girls died in World War." *The New York Times.* Nov. 11, 1922.
cliv "Miss Grace Hershey." *The Hope (Kansas) Dispatch.* Nov. 7, 1918.

CHAPTER 6
clv Brooks, Michelle. Page on Emma Colgan. Ancestry.com.
clvi Schwartz, Thomas. Story of Daniel Colgan Sr. Ancestry.com.
clvii "Bryan, William S. and Robert Rose. *A History of Pioneer Families in Missouri.* Bryan, Brand & Co., St. Louis. P143-144. 1876.
clviii Ibid.
clix Ibid.
clx Schwartz, Thomas. Story of Robert "Bob" Colgan Sr. Ancestry.com.
clxi Schwartz, Thomas. "Mott Family Notes." Unpublished.
clxii Tyson, Robert A. *History of East St. Louis: Its Resources, Statistics, Railroads, Physical Features, Business and Advantages.* J. Haps & Company. P110. 1875.
clxiii U.S., War of 1812 Service Records, 1812-1815. Service of Alfred Sanford. Ancestry.com.
clxiv Brooks, Michelle. Page on Scioto Sanford. Ancestry.com.
clxv Brooks, Michelle. Page on Orphena Sanford. Ancestry.com.
clxvi *Missouri State Times* (Jefferson City, Mo.). Aug. 18, 1865.
clxvii *Central Missourian* (California, Mo.). Aug. 10, 1867.
clxviii *People's Tribune* (Jefferson City, Mo.). Feb. 8, 1871.
clxix *State Journal* (Jefferson City, Mo.). May 29, 1874.
clxx *People's Tribune* (Jefferson City, Mo.). Jan 27, 1875.
clxxi *State Journal* (Jefferson City, Mo.). Dec. 12, 1873.
clxxii *Canton Press.* Dec. 26, 1884.
clxxiii *People's Tribune* (Jefferson City, Mo.). Sept. 8, 1875.
clxxiv *People's Tribune* (Jefferson City, Mo.). March 18, 1875.
clxxv Gelbert, Doug. *Look Up, Jefferson City! A Walking Tour of Jefferson City, Missouri.* Look Up, America! Series. Cruden Bay Books. 2012.
clxxvi *Jefferson Inquirer* (Jefferson City, Mo.). June 4, 1859.
clxxvii *People's Tribune* (Jefferson City, Mo.). April 21, 1875; May 31, 1871. *State Republican* (Jefferson City, Mo.). March 12, 1891.
clxxviii Keller, Rudi. "150 Years Ago: Emancipation supporters fail in effort to call new state convention." *Columbia Tribune.* March 21, 2013.
clxxix *People's Tribune* (Jefferson City, Mo.). Dec. 4, 1872.
clxxx *Sedalia Weekly Bazoo.* Feb. 22, 1887.

[clxxxi] Ford. 1938.

[clxxxii] *Sedalia Weekly Bazoo*. Feb. 22, 1887.

[clxxxiii] *People's Tribune* (Jefferson City). Feb. 13, 1867.

[clxxxiv] Ford. 1938.

[clxxxv] *St. Louis Globe Democrat*. Dec. 19, 1884.

[clxxxvi] Missouri, Wills and Probate Records, 1766-1988 (Cole County). Ancestry.com.

[clxxxvii] *Jefferson City Daily Press*. June 7, 1899.

[clxxxviii] Biographical Sketches of Early Cole County Residents. About George Porth. www.colecohistsoc.org

CHAPTER 7

[clxxxix] Owens, Loretta E. "Mrs. William Logan Bennett 92 years young." *The Lincoln Clarion* (Jefferson City, Mo.). Oct. 22, 1943.

[cxc] Ibid.

[cxci] "Civil War Pension Files." Fold3.com. Service of Byron Hess. National Archives, Washington, D.C.

[cxcii] Richardson, Joe M. "The American Missionary Association and Black Education in Civil War Missouri." *Missouri Historical Review*. July 1975.

[cxciii] Ibid.

[cxciv] Ibid.

[cxcv] Ibid.

[cxcvi] Ibid.

[cxcvii] Ibid.

[cxcviii] Montague, Lydia. Letter to Rev. S.S. Jocelyn dated Jan. 27, 1864. American Missionary Association archives, Amistad Research Center, New Orleans, La.

[cxcix] Montague, Lydia. Letter to Rev. S.S. Jocelyn dated April 26, 1864. American Missionary Association archives, Amistad Research Center, New Orleans, La.

[cc] Ibid.

[cci] Richardson. July 1975.

[ccii] Montague, Lydia. Report to Rev. G. Whipple dated June 24, 1864. American Missionary Association archives, Amistad Research Center, New Orleans, La.

[cciii] Montague, Lydia. Letter to Rev. Ptrechy dated June 20, 1864. American Missionary Association archives, Amistad Research Center, New Orleans, La.

[cciv] Ibid.

[ccv] Beilein, Joseph M.; Hulbert, Matthew C. *The Civil War Guerrilla: Unfolding the Black Flag in History, Memory, and Myth*. University Press of Kentucky. 2015.

[ccvi] Montague. June 20, 1864.

[ccvii] Richardson. July 1975.

[ccviii] Montague. June 20, 1864.

[ccix] Montague, Lydia. Letter to Rev. Jocelyn dated July 28, 1864. American Missionary Association archives, Amistad Research Center, New Orleans, La.

[ccx] Montague. June 20, 1864.

[ccxi] Ibid.

[ccxii] Montague, Lydia. July 1864 report to American Missionary Association. American Missionary Association archives, Amistad Research Center, New Orleans, La.

[ccxiii] Hess, Lydia. Letter to Rev. Whipple dated Aug. 4, 1864. American Missionary Association archives, Amistad Research Center, New Orleans, La.

ccxiv Ibid.

ccxv Ibid.

ccxvi Montague. June 20, 1864.

ccxvii Ibid.

ccxviii Montague. June 24, 1864.

ccxix Ibid.

ccxx Ibid.

ccxxi Ibid.

ccxxii Montague. June 20, 1864.

ccxxiii Montague. July 28, 1864.

ccxxiv Montague. June 24, 1864.

ccxxv Ibid.

ccxxvi Montague. July 28, 1864. U.S. Census 1860.

ccxxvii *Examiner*. May 8, 1861.

ccxxviii Montague. July 28, 1864.

ccxxix Ibid.

ccxxx Ibid.

ccxxxi Ibid.

ccxxxii Ibid.

ccxxxiii Ibid.

ccxxxiv Ibid.

ccxxxv Ibid.

ccxxxvi Ibid.

ccxxxvii Montague, Lydia. Letter to Rev. Whipple dated Sept. 7, 1864. American Missionary Association archives, Amistad Research Center, New Orleans, La.

ccxxxviii Montague, Lydia. Letter to Rev. George Whipple dated Nov. 19, 1864. American Missionary Association archives, Amistad Research Center, New Orleans, La.

ccxxxix Ibid.

ccxl Ibid.

ccxli Montague, Lydia. Letter to Rev. L.L. Jocelyn dated Oct. 8, 1864. American Missionary Association archives, Amistad Research Center, New Orleans, La.

ccxlii Montague, Lydia. Letter dated Feb. 2, 1865. American Missionary Association archives, Amistad Research Center, New Orleans, La.

ccxliii Montague, Lydia. Letter to Rev. George Whipple dated Dec. 29, 1864. American Missionary Association archives, Amistad Research Center, New Orleans, La.

ccxliv Montague, Lydia. Letter to Rev. Streby dated March 19, 1865. American Missionary Association archives, Amistad Research Center, New Orleans, La.

ccxlv Ibid.

ccxlvi Ibid.

ccxlvii Ibid.

ccxlviii Ibid.

ccxlix Ibid.

ccl Ibid.

ccli Montague, Lydia. Report to Rev. George Whipple dated Aug. 28, 1865. American Missionary Association archives, Amistad Research Center, New Orleans, La.

cclii Montague, Lydia. Report to Rev. George Whipple dated Aug. 31, 1865. American Missionary Association archives, Amistad Research Center, New Orleans, La.

ccliii Ibid.

ccliv Ibid.

cclv Ibid.

cclvi Ibid.

cclvii Bishop, William. Letter to Rev. George Whipple dated Sept. 2, 1865. American Missionary Association archives, Amistad Research Center, New Orleans, La.

cclviii Ibid.

cclix Ibid.

cclx Ibid.

cclxi Montague. March 19, 1865.

cclxii Montague. Aug. 28, 1865.

cclxiii Montague, Lydia. Letter to Rev. L.L. Jocelyn dated May 28, 1865. American Missionary Association archives, Amistad Research Center, New Orleans, La.

cclxiv Montague, Lydia. Letter to Rev. M.E. Streby dated June 13, 1865. American Missionary Association archives, Amistad Research Center, New Orleans, La.

cclxv Montague. May 28, 1865.

cclxvi Montague. June 13, 1865.

cclxvii Montague. Aug. 28, 1865.

cclxviii Montague. June 13, 1865.

cclxix Montague. Aug. 31, 1865.

cclxx Montague, Lydia. Report to Rev. G. Whipple dated Feb. 17, 1866. American Missionary Association archives, Amistad Research Center, New Orleans, La.

cclxxi Ibid.

cclxxii Ibid.

cclxxiii Ibid.

cclxxiv Montague, Lydia. Report to Rev. J. Hunt dated May 28, 1866. American Missionary Association archives, Amistad Research Center, New Orleans, La.

cclxxv Montague, Lydia. Report to Rev. J. Hunt dated June 3, 1866. American Missionary Association archives, Amistad Research Center, New Orleans, La.

cclxxvi U.S. School Catalogs 1765-1935. Record for Esther Ann Buffington. Ancestry.com.

cclxxvii U.S. Quaker Meeting Records, 1681-1935. Record for Esther Ann Buffington. Ancestry.com.

cclxxviii Montague, Lydia. Report to Rev. George Whipple dated Dec. 5, 1867. American Missionary Association archives, Amistad Research Center, New Orleans, La.

cclxxix Ibid.

cclxxx *The Carthage Press*. Jan. 25, 1902.

cclxxxi Foster, Richard Baxter. *Lincoln University Historical Sketch*. Lincoln University Archive.

cclxxxii Montague, Lydia. Report to Rev. George Whipple dated Dec. 5, 1867. American Missionary Association archives, Amistad Research Center, New Orleans, La.

cclxxxiii Montague. June 20, 1864.

cclxxxiv Montague. July 28, 1864.

cclxxxv *St. Louis Globe Democrat* Aug. 31, 1878.

CHAPTER 8

cclxxxvi Brooks, Michelle. Page on Estella F. Branham. Ancestry.com.

cclxxxvii 68th U.S. Colored Troops Description List. Fold3.com. Service of George W.

Branham. National Archives. Washington D.C.

cclxxxviii U.S. Widow's Pension Applications. Application of America Branham Longley. National Archives. Washington D.C.

cclxxxix Brooks, Michelle. Page on George W. Branham. Ancestry.com.

ccxc U.S. Widow's Pension Applications. Application of America Branham Longley. National Archives. Washington D.C.

ccxci Ibid.

ccxcii *Lincoln Clarion* (Jefferson City, Mo.). March 9, 1949.

ccxciii *Jefferson City Post-Tribune*. Feb. 28, 1949.

ccxciv Brooks, Michelle. Page on Frances 'Fannie' Arnold. Ancestry.com.

ccxcv *Jefferson City Post-Tribune*. Oct. 8, 1970.

ccxcvi *Sunday News-Tribune (Jefferson City, Mo.)*. Oct. 18, 1970.

ccxcvii *Lincoln Clarion* (Jefferson City, Mo.). Feb. 20, 1953.

ccxcviii *Jefferson City Post-Tribune*. Oct. 8, 1970.

ccxcix *Kansas City Journal*. Sept. 27, 1896.

ccc *Word and Way* (Kansas City). April 29, 1948.

ccci *Lincoln Clarion* (Jefferson City, Mo.). Oct. 26, 1945.

cccii *Kansas City Star*. Oct. 1, 1949.

ccciii *Word and Way* (Kansas City). May 25, 1950.

ccciv *Lincoln Clarion* (Jefferson City, Mo.). Oct. 24, 1947. Sylvia Morris Ferguson interview with Janet Gallaher for Historic City of Jefferson oral history project, May 8, 2017.

cccv *Lincoln Clarion* (Jefferson City, Mo.). Oct. 24, 1947.

cccvi Ibid.

cccvii Duke Diggs Jefferson City Photograph Collection finding aid. Manuscript Collections. Missouri State Archive, Jefferson City, Mo.

cccviii Ibid.

cccix Ibid.

cccx *The Rising Son* (Kansas City). Aug. 17, 1907.

cccxi "United Brothers of Friendship and Sisters of the Mysterious Ten." Freemasonry and Fraternal Organizations. Stichting Argus Foundation. www.stichtingargus.nl/vrijmetselarij/ubfsmt_en.html.

cccxii Ibid.

cccxiii *The Rising Son* (Kansas City). Aug. 17, 1907.

cccxiv Ibid.

cccxv *Daily Capital News* (Jefferson City, Mo.). Aug. 26, 1934.

cccxvi Ibid.

cccxvii Sylvia Morris Ferguson interview with Janet Gallaher for Historic City of Jefferson oral history project, May 8, 2017.

cccxviii *Lincoln Clarion* (Jefferson City, Mo.). Jan. 15, 1954. Sylvia Morris Ferguson interview with Janet Gallaher for Historic City of Jefferson oral history project, May 8, 2017.

cccxix "The Jefferson City Community Center." National Register of Historic Places nomination. (U.S Department of the Interior, National Parks Service.) 1992.

cccxx *Sunday News Tribune* (Jefferson City, Mo.). Nov. 24, 1946.

cccxxi *Sunday News Tribune* (Jefferson City, Mo.). Feb. 18, 1951.

cccxxii Ibid.

cccxxiii *Lincoln Clarion* (Jefferson City, Mo.). May 2, 1952.

cccxxiv Ibid.

cccxxv *Moberly Monitor Index*. April 4, 1944.

cccxxvi *Daily Capital News* (Jefferson City, Mo.). April 4, 1944.

cccxxvii Ibid.

cccxxviii Ibid.

cccxxix Ibid.

cccxxx *Lincoln Clarion* (Jefferson City, Mo.). March 28, 1947.

cccxxxi Sylvia Morris Ferguson interview with Janet Gallaher for Historic City of Jefferson oral history project, May 8, 2017.

cccxxxii Ibid.

cccxxxiii Ibid.

cccxxxiv Ibid.

cccxxxv *Lincoln Clarion* (Jefferson City, Mo.). Oct. 26, 1945.

CHAPTER 9

cccxxxvi Schreiber, Mark. *Somewhere In Time: 170 Year of Missouri Corrections*. Walsworth Publishing Company, Marceline. 2004.

cccxxxvii Norfleet, Don. "Jere Giffen: Journalist, educator, author and volunteer." Active Times. *The Jefferson City News Tribune*. Oct. 7, 2001.

cccxxxviii Ibid.

cccxxxix Ibid.

cccxl Schreiber. 2004.

cccxli Ibid.

cccxlii Norfleet. 2001.

cccxliii Ibid.

cccxliv Ibid.

cccxlv Marson. Page on Jerena "Jere" East Giffen. Findagrave.com.

cccxlvi Ibid.

cccxlvii Ibid.

cccxlviii "Kidnap-Killers Die Side by Side Amid Swirling Clouds of Cyanide." *Jefferson City Post-Tribune*. Dec. 18, 1953.

cccxlix Norfleet. 2001

cccl Ibid.

cccli "Kidnap-Killers Die Side by Side." 1953.

ccclii Ibid.

cccliii Norfleet. 2001

cccliv Ibid.

ccclv Ibid.

ccclvi Ibid.

ccclvii Ibid.

ccclviii Ibid.

ccclix Giffen. Obituaries. *Jefferson City Post-Tribune*. March 2, 1999.

ccclx Ibid.

ccclxi Reagan, Michelle. "Jere Giffen: Nose for news on Jefferson City history." Undated. *Jefferson City News Tribune.*

ccclxii Gaynor, Steve. "Real life: Poli sci professor has experienced what she teaches."

Rolla Daily News. Dec. 6, 1990.

ccclxiii Marson. Page on Jerena "Jere" East Giffen. Findagrave.com.

ccclxiv Giffen, Dr. Lawrence. Letter to friends. May 1, 1969. Missouri State Historical Society, Columbia.

ccclxv Gaynor. 1990.

ccclxvi Ibid.

ccclxvii Ibid.

ccclxviii Giffen, Jerena East, Papers, 1893-2008. Missouri State Historical Society, Columbia. 2000.

ccclxix Reagan. Undated.

ccclxx Ibid.

ccclxxi Ibid.

ccclxxii Ibid.

ccclxxiii Pearson, Les. "First Ladies of Missouri." Family. *The Globe-Democrat* (St. Louis). May 25, 1970.

ccclxxiv The Missouri Writers' Guild News. April 1971.

ccclxxv Giffen, Lawrence Everett. "Walks in Water: Steamboating on the Lower Missouri River." Giffen Enterprises. 2001. Manuscripts Collection. Missouri State Archive.

ccclxxvi Marson. Page on Jerena "Jere" East Giffen. Findagrave.com..

ccclxxvii Brownlee Fund Grant Recipients. State Historical Society of Missouri. 2002.

ccclxxviii Giffen, Jerena East. *Mary, Mary Quite … The Life and Times of Mary Whitney Phelps 1812-1878*. Giffen Enterprises. 2008.

ccclxxix Giffen, Jerena East. Letter to Sam B. Cook. 2005.

ccclxxx Giffen, Jerena East. *Smile - There's a Rainbow: The Insight of Spy Dry*. Giffen Enterprises. 2009.

ccclxxxi Marson. Page on Jerena "Jere" East Giffen. Findagrave.com.

CHAPTER 10

ccclxxxii Brooks, Michelle. Page on Sarah Mildred Parsons. Ancestry.com.

ccclxxxiii Brooks Michelle. Page on Gen. Gustavus Adolphus Parsons. Ancestry.com.

ccclxxxiv Ibid.

ccclxxxv Hobbs, Myrene. Letter by Mildred Standish. *Daily Capital News* (Jefferson City). March 20, 1942.

ccclxxxvi *Jefferson Inquirer*. Oct. 10, 1844.

ccclxxxvii Brooks, Michelle. "Parsons Home: Home to history." *Jefferson City News-Tribune*. March 15, 2009.

ccclxxxviii Ibid.

ccclxxxix Hobbs. 1942.

cccxc Connelley, William Elsey. Hughes, John Taylor. *War with Mexico, 1846-47: Doniphan's Expedition and the conquest of New Mexico and California*. Heritage Books. 2009.

cccxci 1850 U.S. Census. Cole County, Missouri. Page 1B.

cccxcii Brooks. 2009.

cccxciii Young, Dr. Robert. *Pioneers of High, Water and Main: Reflections of Jefferson City*. Twelfth State. 1997.

cccxciv Ibid.

cccxcv Brooks, Michelle. Page on Henry 'Duncan' Lynn. Ancestry.com.

cccxcvi Standish, Austin. Letter on Missouri State Penitentiary stationery. Mosby Monroe Parsons Papers. Missouri Historical Society, St. Louis.

cccxcvii Connelley.2009.

cccxcviii Ibid.

cccxcix 1860 U.S. Census. Jefferson City, Cole County, Missouri. Page 383.

cd Brooks. 2009.

cdi Parsons, Mosby Monroe. Letter to son Kearney. Mosby Monroe Parsons Papers. Missouri Historical Society, St. Louis.

cdii General Order #2. Headquarters Purdall's Sharpshooters. Mosby Monroe Parsons Papers. Missouri Historical Society, St. Louis.

cdiii Ibid.

cdiv Standish, Austin. Letter on Missouri State Penitentiary stationery. Mosby Monroe Parsons Papers. Missouri Historical Society, St. Louis.

cdv Hewitt, Lawrence L. Arthur W. Bergeron. Thomas E. Schott. *Confederate General in the Trans-Mississippi: Volume 1: Essays on America's Civil War.* University of Tennessee Press. 2013.

cdvi Connelley. 2009.

cdvii Hobbs. 1942.

cdviii Ibid.

cdix Ibid.

cdx Ibid.

cdxi Ibid.

cdxii Ibid.

cdxiii Ibid.

cdxiv Ibid.

cdxv Ibid.

cdxvi Ibid.

cdxvii Ibid.

cdxviii Ibid.

cdxix Ibid.

cdxx Ibid.

cdxxi Ibid.

cdxxii Ibid.

cdxxiii Ibid.

cdxxiv Ibid.

cdxxv Ibid.

cdxxvi Ibid.

cdxxvii Musser, R.H. "The Death of General M.M. Parsons. From *Jefferson City Daily Tribune*, Feb. 2, 1886. Missouri History Not Found in Textbooks. *The Missouri Historical Review.* Vol. 31. No. 4. July 1937.

cdxxviii Standish, Mildred Parsons. Folder 11. Mosby Monroe Parsons Papers. Missouri Historical Society, St. Louis.

cdxxix Denslow, Ray V. *Civil War and Masonry in Missouri.* Literary Licensing, LLC. 2011.

cdxxx Hobbs. 1942.

cdxxxi Parsons, Mosby M. Letter to Gustavus and Patience Parsons. June 5, 1865. Mosby Monroe Parsons Papers. Missouri Historical Society, St. Louis.

cdxxxii Ibid.

cdxxxiii Hobbs. 1942.

cdxxxiv Ibid.

cdxxxv Ibid.

cdxxxvi Standish, Mildred Parsons. Folder 11. Mosby Monroe Parsons Papers. Missouri Historical Society, St. Louis.

cdxxxvii Hobbs. 1942.

cdxxxviii *Daily Capital News* (Jefferson City, Mo.). May 25, 1919.

cdxxxix Musser. July 1937.

cdxl Ibid.

cdxli Ibid.

cdxlii Ibid.

cdxliii *Kansas City Journal*. Dec. 7, 1898.

cdxliv *People's Tribune* (Jefferson City, Mo.). June 24, 1874.

cdxlv *Kansas City Times*. Sept. 3, 1875.

cdxlvi *People's Tribune* (Jefferson City, Mo.). June 24, 1874.

cdxlvii *People's Tribune* (Jefferson City, Mo.). June 24, 1874.

cdxlviii *Kansas City Times*. Sept. 3, 1875.

cdxlix *Kansas City Times*. Sept. 3, 1875.

cdl *People's Tribune* (Jefferson City, Mo.). June 24, 1874.

cdli *People's Tribune* (Jefferson City, Mo.). June 24, 1874.

cdlii Moore, John Bassett. *History and Digest of International Arbitration*. P. 3004. 1898.

cdliii *People's Tribune* (Jefferson City, Mo.). June 24, 1874.

cdliv Moore. 1898.

cdlv Ibid. Brooks, Michelle. Page on Aaron Conrow. Ancestry.com.

cdlvi *Cole County Democrat* (Jefferson City, Mo.). Jan. 25, 1889.

cdlvii 1870 U.S. Census. Jefferson, Cole County, Missouri. Page 231A.

cdlviii *St. Louis Globe Democrat*. Dec. 16, 1877.

cdlix Ibid.

cdlx Missouri School for the Blind collection. Missouri State Archive, Jefferson City, Missouri.

cdlxi *People's Tribune* (Jefferson City, Mo.). Jan. 18, 1882.

cdlxii Ibid.

cdlxiii *Cole County Democrat* (Jefferson City, Mo.). Oct. 3, 1884.

cdlxiv "A Good Woman Gone." *Jefferson City Daily State Journal*. Jan. 31, 1884.

cdlxv Brooks, Michelle. Page on Dr. Austin D'Arcy Standish. Ancestry.com.

cdlxvi Ibid.

cdlxvii Brooks, Michelle. Page on Monroe Parsons Standish. Ancestry.com.

cdlxviii Brooks, Michelle. Page on Sarah Mildred Parsons. Ancestry.com.

cdlxix "Daughters of the Confederacy." *St. Louis Globe Democrat*. July 19, 1898.

cdlxx Ibid.

cdlxxi *Lincoln (Nebraska) Star*. Dec. 27, 1908.

cdlxxii Associated Press. "Fire destroys St. Mary's Hospital in Jeff City." *Springfield (Missouri) News-Leader*. Feb. 21, 1919.

cdlxxiii *St. Louis Globe Democrat*. March 9, 1919.

cdlxxiv *Daily Capital News* (Jefferson City, Mo.). May 25, 1919.

cdlxxv "Missouri, Andrew and Cole County Probate Records, 1826-1945," images, FamilySearch.org. Cole, estate of Standish, Mildred Parsons. Missouri State Archive,

Jefferson City, Mo.
cdlxxvi *Daily Capital News* (Jefferson City, Mo.). March 20, 1942.

Made in the USA
Columbia, SC
24 September 2022

67524497R00057